Warrior

Ageless Wisdom for

To Andrew —

May you always live
with honor!

Bohdi Sanders

Warrior Wisdom

Ageless Wisdom for the Modern Warrior

Bohdi Sanders, PhD

Updated Second Edition

Published by Kaizen Quest Publishing

Printed in the United States of America

Library of Congress Cataloging-in-Publication Data
Sanders, Bohdi, 1962-
Warrior Wisdom: Ageless Wisdom for the Modern Warrior

ISBN - 978-1-937884-00-0

1. Martial Arts. 2. Self-Help. 3. Philosophy. I. Title

Acknowledgements

This book is dedicated to the most amazing wife in the world, my wife Tracey, for the total support that she has always given me. No matter what the endeavor, she has always been behind me 100%. I cannot imagine a more supportive wife. Without her endless support and patience, this book would not have been possible. I am truly a very lucky man, thank you sweetheart.

And to, Faith Lester and Alpine Photography for the great job she did with the photography for *Warrior Wisdom* and a very special thank you to my little buddy and model Jacob Lester for his time and cooperation in making the photo shoot a success.

And finally, but certainly not least, I would like to thank the following individuals for the encouragement and endorsement of *Warrior Wisdom*.

Lawrence Kane

Alain Burrese

Peyton Quinn

Dr. Kevin Keough

Marc MacYoung

Cherokee Parks

Wim Demeere

About the Author

Bohdi Sanders is a lifelong student of wisdom literature, the healing arts, and the martial arts. His studies led him to explore the wisdom behind natural health, naturopathy, herbs, Reiki, Qigong, meditation, and the power of the mind to heal the body and to make positive changes in one's life. These explorations led to him earning doctorate degrees in naturopathy and in natural health.

Dr. Sanders is also a Certified Personal Fitness Trainer, a Certified Specialist in Martial Arts Conditioning, a Certified Reiki Master, and a Certified Master of G-Jo Acupressure. He holds a black belt in Shotokan Karate and has studied various other martial arts for over 30 years. He has worked with young people for over 20 years and is endorsed to teach in five different subject areas. He is the author of:

- *Warrior Wisdom: Ageless Wisdom for the Modern Warrior*
- *Warrior Wisdom: The Heart and Soul of Bushido*
- *The Warrior Lifestyle: Making Your Life Extraordinary*
- *The Secrets of Worldly Wisdom*
- *Secrets of the Soul*
- *Wisdom of the Elders*
- *Modern Bushido: Living a Life of Excellence*

Dr. Sanders' books have received high praise and have won several national awards, including:

- The Indie Excellence Book Awards: 1st Place Winner 2010
- USA Book News Best Books of 2010: 1st Place Winner 2010
- IIMAA: Best Martial Arts Book of the Year 2011
- USA Martial Arts HOF: Literary Man of the Year 2011
- U. S. Martial Artist Association: Inspiration of the Year 2011
- U. S. Martial Arts Hall of Fame: Author of the Year 2011

www.TheWisdomWarrior.com

Endorsements for Warrior Wisdom

To be candid, when I was first approached about reviewing Dr. Sanders' manuscript, *Warrior Wisdom*, I was somewhat apprehensive. Not from any preconceived notion about him as an author, but rather from my experience as a reader. I've read dozens of martial arts philosophy books over the years and have found the majority to be pedantic and entirely forgettable.

I considered, however, how hard I worked to get testimonials for my first couple of books and decided that I ought to do a new author a favor by at least taking a look at his work. After reading Sanders' manuscript, however, it turns out that it was he who did me the favor, not the other way around. His book is not only memorable, but thought-provoking and insightful as well. I'm honored to be among the first few people to have read it.

Warrior Wisdom is a pithy book. While you could easily read the whole thing from cover to cover in a couple hours as I did the first time through, I believe that it is better to pick a page or two a day and spend some time absorbing what you have read. The 167 quotations could easily stand alone, yet the author's succinct commentaries add far more to the reading experience than their length would suggest. He helps you digest the information, understand the essence of warriorhood, and explore your own character as it relates to the topic. With a little "think time" some of the sections can be quite profound.

As the Japanese poet Basho (1644 – 1694) wrote, "Do not seek to follow in the footsteps of wise men, seek what they sought." In other words don't focus overmuch on the person but rather on what made him (or her) great. Sanders' book is an excellent resource for doing just that. It is a thinking person's guide to development as a martial artist, warrior, and human being. And, it's something worth reading more than once.

Lawrence Kane

Author of: *Surviving Armed Assaults* and *Martial Arts Instruction*; co- author of *The Way of Kata*, *The Way to Black Belt*, and *The Little Black Book of Violence*.

Endorsements for Warrior Wisdom

Bohdi Sanders' book *Warrior Wisdom* bridges the gap between ageless wisdom and modern application for today's warriors. Dr. Sanders writes that being a warrior is not something you do; it is something you are. In this book, he provides the guidance to live and be a warrior physically, mentally, and physically.

In fact, his lessons on honor, responsibility, wisdom, courage, and most importantly character, are what will make this book an excellent contribution to any library, especially that of the martial artist. I agree with Sanders that it takes much more to be a real warrior than spending time in a martial arts class or being in the military, and I appreciated his focus on character and self-discipline.

The value in this unique book lies in the commentary on warriorship by Sanders which is inspired by classic quotes on the warrior way. These lessons not only form a road map toward martial success, but to success in all your daily activities. A lifestyle committed to the ideals of warriorship is powerful, and for those who commit to the holistic discipline aimed at the pursuit of excellence, not just in the training hall, but at life, know that even though it takes effort to live the way of the warrior, it is worth it.

Warrior Wisdom is filled with stimulating quotes, valuable insights, and inspiring examples of how a warrior should train, act, and live. Use the text to help develop and shape your own warrior code of honor, your moral compass pointing toward what is right and just. Make these warrior ideals a permanent part of your character and be someone who achieves in any field of endeavor.

This book will be an invaluable resource for anyone following the warrior's path or who desires to live the warrior way. Don't just study and learn from this book, apply the wisdom and live it. A must read for those who consider themselves warriors and live by the values of honor, courage, and commitment.

Alain Burrese, J.D.

Author of: *Hard Won Wisdom From the School of Hard Knocks* and the instructional DVD's *Hapkido Hoshinsul, Streetfighting Essentials, Hapkido Cane & Lock On: Joint Locking Essentials* series.

Endorsements for Warrior Wisdom

Warrior Wisdom is not a "technique book." Do we really need yet another "technique-based" book anyway? The correct answer is, "NO, not likely." However, I do recommend you read *Warrior Wisdom* as it isn't about physical technique, which in my experience is not the total "answer" in self-defense that people often mistake it for either.

Bohdi Sanders' book is about the mental "technique" that is the warrior mindset. He dissects scores of classical martial sayings and brings them into the clarity of our modern life. I think for many people when they read this work, they will realize a new and functional insight they did not previously enjoy, even though they may have heard the "saying" before.

Most of all Bohdi Sanders' work puts forth the main and most essential important principle of "thinking and living in a martial manner." He expresses that principle economically and yet quite directly "The Martial Way does not stop and start at the door of the training hall. It is a way of life in every action, in and out of the training hall, and is done in the context of warriorship."

You must endeavor to truly understand this reality in order to follow your truest and best path. *Warrior Wisdom* is a fine tool to help you find that understanding in all its depth.

"Buy it, read it, live it."

Peyton Quinn

Author of: *A Bouncer's Guide to Barroom Brawling, Freedom from Fear*, and *Real Fighting: Adrenaline Stress Conditioning Through Scenario- Based Training*.

Endorsements for Warrior Wisdom

It is relatively uncommon to stumble upon a book that most everyone will find interesting and inspiring. Readers are introduced to an exceptional blend of cross-cultural and timeless wisdom. Each page contains truly classic proverbs and gems of wisdom combined with insightful commentary that leads readers to a recognition of the practical and immediate relevance of ancient wisdom in our 21st century lives.

Dr. Sanders demonstrates a remarkable understanding of young people and seekers of all ages in the careful selection and down to earth discussion of ideas that will enrich their lives. This book is a gift that keeps on giving as each page heightens awareness of the best within us and a solidarity that forever unites.

While reading *Warrior Wisdom*, an old Native American Seneca saying remained with me; "When the wisdom-keepers speak, all should listen."

Dr. Kevin Keough

Clinical and police psychologist, martial artist, founder of Warrior Traditions, and fellow pilgrim.

Warrior Wisdom is proof that "dynamite comes in small packages". Dr. Sanders has assimilated the wisdom of the ages, which defines what it means to be an ethical, responsible, and honorable person, not just a warrior, into a guide that is applicable to everyone, not just Martial Artists.

By using simple, yet painstakingly accurate, explanations of the gems of wisdom passed down to us from a thousand years of intellect, he has crafted an excellent guide for the application of that wisdom…it should be required reading for all in the hopes that it would become a guide to adulthood, for both those already there and those yet to become adults. I applaud you, Dr. Sanders, for your contribution to mankind.

Cherokee Parks

Author of: *Hard Ride to Cora* and *Jake Laughlin's Second Bath in the Same Year.*

Endorsements for Warrior Wisdom

Warrior Wisdom is a great book for everybody who chooses to live the martial way. Regardless of the martial art you train in or the self-defense system you practice, this book has valuable information for you. But especially for LEO's and soldiers; the nuggets of wisdom in these pages hold tremendous value. Simply because they help you think about the life you chose – that of a warrior.

Warriors live an unusual life and are confronted with situations most people haven't even heard of. By meditating on the quotes in this book, they can get a better understanding of their own lives and how to interact with "civilians," for lack of a better word.

You get the most out of this book by reading a few pages and then thinking about the implications of the information in your own life. Even if you don't agree with the conclusion, at least you'll have reaffirmed your own position. But in many cases, you'll find the words inspiring and comforting. Highly recommended!

Wim Demeere

Author of: *The Fighter's Body, Exercise and Excellence in the Martial Arts, Timing in the Fighting Arts,* and *The Fighter's Guide to Hard-Core Heavy Bag Training.*

Foreword

This foreword begins with a warrior asking me for a favor. A few years ago my phone rang and it was Andrew Vachss on the other end of the line. Now in case you don't know who he is, that man is a warrior. Although the battles he now fights are legal and legislative, he's no stranger to bloodshed and violence. He had a favor to ask me. He asked, "Could you say in your next book how beating children is NOT how a warrior behaves? It would carry a lot of weight coming from a heavy hitter like you."

On one hand I was honored that such a warrior and man whose crusade I strongly support would ask this of me. On the other I was stunned that I had never thought about such an obvious thing to say. I had known this and the other issues, which I will talk about next, for years. But it wasn't until Vachss' call that I began to put them together in a different perspective.

To me child and spousal abuse is reprehensible; something that automatically triggers a berserk charge to stop it. Contrary to popular myths, people who do violence to their family are seldom cowards. In fact, I've had some hard fights coming from stopping such violence. What was always surprising was the self-righteous fury that these people fought with. And that is something that is worth considering.

I've met child and wife beaters who don't have the vaguest idea that what they are doing is worse than wrong, they only have one answer to any of life's problems and that is violence. And they will fight you with every ounce of power they have.

With that in mind, I'd like you to consider this question: What does it mean to be a warrior?

The simple fact is that I have met many people, who claim to be warriors, who are basically loose cannons on deck. The reason for this is that it is they - and they alone - who decide that they are "warriors." As the sole arbitrator of this standard, they can conveniently pick and choose what it means to be a warrior. Some of their choices, I have had to deal with, like the guy who wanted to duel someone over an insult to a lady. A lady, who was not only capable of handling the problem herself, but hadn't been insulted at all; to her it was just a joke.

And yet, here was a guy who claimed to be a warrior but was intent on violence for no other reason than what he felt. He had decided the woman was wronged. He refused to listen to others, including the woman herself (who tried to explain to him that it was a running joke between her and the group). He didn't care what the social dynamic was, he had decided to use the threat of force to compel others to behaving the way he wanted them to.

Here is a real short hand answer to, "what does it mean to be a warrior?" Being a warrior is about protecting others, not picking and choosing where and when you will fight.

That man, instead of protecting the group, became a threat to it. And he had become a threat to it because he had lost the bigger perspective of what it means to be a warrior, being a protector, not a threat. The simple truth is warriors are not looked upon in high regard in this society. And the reason is that the line between a warrior and an abuser is as small as losing sight of the bigger picture.

If you look at a warrior as someone who serves the whole of society then you will begin to see how it can begin to go wrong when that scope is narrowed. A warrior who only serves to protect a particular power cabal becomes an oppressor. A person who serves no one but his own selfish goals, impulses and desires is not a warrior; he's just another violent abuser or criminal. Someone who brings with him the threat of violence with no predictability as to when and where he will unleash it is not a warrior.

And that idea scares the very people the warrior lives to protect.

If your choice to be a warrior scares people, then something is wrong. This is something you must examine closely. Perhaps it is because there is too much selfishness in your decisions to deploy force. Perhaps it is because you have not communicated to people that you are there to protect them, not harm them. Perhaps it is because in their past they have been abused by someone using violence for selfish ends and they have no understanding that is not what you do. Perhaps it is because they are up to something that they know you will stop if you discover their activities.

Being a warrior doesn't mean just fighting, it requires you to think and observe. It requires a higher level of awareness and understanding. And once you are sure, then it requires action. Unfortunately there are too many people in this world who want the benefits of being a warrior without the cost. Or to be more accurate, they want the perceived benefits.

It is a sad truth that many of the loose cannons who want to call themselves warriors take sadistic delight in inducing fear and discomfort in others. To them, that is a "beanie" of being a warrior.

When I say surety requires action, I mean a true warrior upon realizing that he is unnecessarily scaring someone, he is not afraid to reflect on why. If his behavior is wrong, then he will change it. If it is because the person has been harmed in the past, then he will explain that he is not a danger to that person because, unlike the person who hurt them, he lives his life by a code that prevents him from harming the innocent.

If you choose to walk the warrior's path, then you must always be on guard against forgetting how easy it is to lose sight of the purpose of a warrior. You must always be on guard against you narrowing your vision for convenience or profit. How many warriors by doing so have themselves become the oppressors and abusers? Never, forget, the purpose of a warrior is to serve the whole of society, not just a small section. Warriors serve the greater good and not simply themselves.

This book addresses many of the life issues that you will have to sit down, think about and come up with a strategy that not only works for you, but with other people. The value of this book isn't that it will teach you HOW to be a warrior. Nor will it teach you how to go forward when everyone else is running for cover. What it will do is help you get along in life if you're the kind of person who doesn't step backwards with the rest of the line.

Marc "Animal" MacYoung

Author of: *A Professional's Guide to Ending Violence Quickly* and *"Secrets" of Effective Offense: Survival Strategies for Self-Defense, Martial Arts, and Law Enforcement.*

Introduction

What is the warrior lifestyle? The true warrior is a rare person in today's world. He lives life with a different set of values compared with the rest of society. Even those who do share the same values, rarely live a lifestyle which adheres to those values to the extent that the warrior does. To most people, ethics are situational. They make decisions according to what is best for them, instead of what is right. This is not the case with the warrior. The warrior values honor, integrity, justice, and his sense of what is right, above all else. His ethics are not situational; they are his way of life.

The warrior lifestyle revolves around a code of ethics which is non-negotiable. The warrior's code of ethics, or code of honor, is taken very seriously. To the warrior, distinguishing between right and wrong is of the utmost importance. He sees right and wrong in terms of black and white. He knows that an action is either honorable or dishonorable. This is not to imply that honor is black and white; honor is not that simple.

Those who live the lifestyle of the warrior know that whether or not an action is honorable, is determined by both one's intentions and the situation at hand. This is not to be confused with situational ethics. The warrior's ethics do not change according to the situation. His actions will change as needed, but his ethics remain set in stone. There is a big difference between ethics and actions. Ethics determine actions; actions do not determine ethics.

The warrior lifestyle is concerned with what is right and what is honorable. A warrior's ethics revolve around these two issues. Justice and honor are foremost on his mind. His thoughts are centered on "what is right," not on other people's opinions of what is right. He realizes that many people profess a belief in absolutes which they neither live by, nor truly believe in when push comes to shove.

The only absolute the warrior lives by is that which is right and wrong. If it is not right, he doesn't do it. He determines what is right and wrong by his strict code of ethics, not some arbitrary laws or the politically correct standards of the day. The warrior doesn't appear to be honorable; he is honorable. Sincerity is ingrained in this lifestyle.

This is a lifestyle that is meant to be lived, not fantasized about or merely discussed.

This lifestyle consists of much more than being trained in the art of war or the art of self-defense, although these are an important part of the life of a warrior. It also consists of the challenge to perfect one's character. This is a process much like the Japanese concept of kaizen. Kaizen can be translated as constant, never-ending improvement. True warriors try to apply this concept to every area of their life. They seek to balance and improve each area: spirit, mind, and body, on a daily basis.

Each area of your life is important and should be kept in balance. Training men in the art of war or in the martial arts, without regard to character, only produces a dangerous man; it does not produce a warrior. In years past, the martial arts masters would not train someone fully until they felt assured of that person's character. Today most schools will train anyone who can pay, regardless of their character or lack thereof. This is dangerous information to give to just any and everyone who comes along. In my opinion, character should be a prerequisite not only for martial arts training, but for many of the privileges which we enjoy in this country.

I am often asked whether or not I believe that the term "warrior" should apply only to military men and women who have been in war, or to trained and experienced fighters. Although I realize that this is the literal definition of a warrior, I do not believe that this is the correct definition, not according to the many accounts from past warriors anyway. This literal definition of a warrior is not the definition that is used for our discussion of the warrior lifestyle in *Warrior Wisdom*. An ape can be trained to throw punches and kicks, a dog can be trained to fight, but that doesn't make either of them warriors. Being a warrior involves more than being trained to fight or being in the military; it involves character training as well. Character training is the true goal of Bushido, the way of the warrior.

Now please don't misunderstand me; I have the utmost respect for our men and women in our military. But I believe that anyone who has ever served in the military will agree that not every soldier lives by the character traits which are necessary for the warrior lifestyle, anymore than every martial artist or every person in general lives by these standards. I am not taking anything away from those who serve our country. Every person who serves our country deserves our respect and gratitude, but service does not necessarily indicate that a person is concerned with perfecting his or her character. It is rare indeed to find people today that take their ethics seriously. It is common to find people who claim to take their ethics seriously, but I am referring to people who "walk the walk," and not merely "talk the talk."

Yes, the warrior is concerned with physical training and the martial arts, but he also knows that character training is the cornerstone of the warrior lifestyle. The true warrior should be trained in the martial arts. His ethics require that he be ready to defend his family, friends, and himself in certain situations. In today's world, you never know when you may have to use your martial arts skills. It is essential that you have this training to be as self-reliant and safe as possible, but without a code of ethics, which based on a deep understanding of what is right and wrong, there is no warrior; there is only someone trained to fight. There is a difference. Without the character traits of honor, integrity, and justice, there is no warrior lifestyle.

In short, the warrior lifestyle is for anyone who wants to live a life of excellence; a life which adheres to a strict code of ethics. You must be willing to live your life based on honor, preparedness, and what is right. This lifestyle requires that you put your ethics before your comfort, and that you put what is right before what is profitable. It requires filial duty, dedication to family and friends, and a willingness to help those in need. It requires independence in thought and action. This lifestyle is a decision, not a profession.

This is just a brief introduction to the lifestyle of the warrior. Each of these points can be greatly expanded and I understand that not everyone will agree with my assessment. Even if you disagree with my definition of a warrior or the characteristics of the warrior lifestyle, you will still find the wisdom in this book to be very useful. *Warrior Wisdom* seeks to provide the reader with wisdom from throughout the ages that will help him live the warrior lifestyle. This lifestyle is not a goal to be achieved, but rather a road to be traveled. It is my fondest wish that this, and the other books in the *Warrior Wisdom* series, help you achieve the warrior lifestyle as you travel down that road with honor and wisdom as your constant companions.

Bohdi Sanders, PhD

WARRIOR WISDOM

1

The student must become a true warrior in an age where there are no more warriors.
Kensho Furuya

Many people believe that the world is full of warriors; after all, almost every country has a military with thousands of men and women trained to go into battle, and thousands more police, firemen, border guards, etc. Thousands of other people take martial arts classes weekly. So the world has to be full of warriors, right? Wrong! The fact is that the true warrior is a rare breed. Becoming a real warrior requires much more than spending time in a martial arts class or being a part of the military or police force.

A true warrior follows a specific lifestyle that revolves around honor, responsibility, wisdom, courage, and character. The warrior lifestyle is not a set of rules for the dojo or a standard of behavior to be used in front of your superiors. It is a lifestyle that cuts to the core of your being; you live it 24/7. It is a lifetime commitment to the ideals of warriorship. Being a warrior is not something you do; it is something that you are.

The aspiring warrior needs to realize that being a true warrior involves much, much more than learning martial arts techniques or being trained in warfare. It involves a total commitment to a new lifestyle, at least new for many people in today's world. This is the lifestyle of warriorship.

2

One must make the warrior walk his everyday walk.
Miyamoto Musashi

Being a warrior is a huge responsibility. Walking the path of the warrior is not something that you can decide to do for a couple of months then take a few days off and come back to it later. To be a true warrior, you have to commit to this lifestyle. The warrior is a warrior, period. He doesn't pretend to be a warrior, he doesn't try to be a warrior, he doesn't want to be a warrior; he *is* a warrior. Therefore, the warrior walk must be his everyday walk, there is no other way.

This does not mean that a warrior has to be in training every minute of every day. In today's world this is impossible for most people. What this does mean is that every day the warrior is living up to the ideals that a warrior should live by, whether he is at work, on vacation, or just relaxing at home. The warrior makes these ideals a permanent part of his character, daily. He lives by his code of honor.

His code of honor dictates his every action. It is his moral compass which points, not north, but towards what is right and just. No two warrior codes are completely alike. The Native Americans say that each man must find his own path, and the same thing applies to the warrior. Each warrior has to determine his own code of honor, but one thing is certain, there is no such thing as the "weekend warrior."

3

Do not be tricked into thinking that there are no crocodiles just because the water is still.
Malaysian Proverb

The majority of people today live a fairly peaceful life. Most of us do not have to defend our lives weekly, monthly, or even yearly. With the exception of law enforcement officers and military men and women, most of us do not have to deal with dangerous criminals or life threatening situations on a daily basis. As a matter of fact, the vast majority of people today will live their entire life without ever encountering a kill-or-be-killed situation. This being the case, you may ask why you should train to be a warrior when the odds are that you will never have to use the skills that you are working so hard to perfect.

The answer is found in the Malaysian proverb above. If you have ever watched one of the wildlife shows on television, you have probably seen how crocodiles attack. An unsuspecting animal, going about his business, stops at a peaceful waterhole for a drink, and out of nowhere the crocodile explodes from the water and ambushes the unsuspecting animal, taking his life.

Don't become complacent with your life or your training. Just because your life seems to be normal and peaceful, doesn't mean that the bad guys aren't out there. Don't make the mistake of believing that "those kinds of things never happen to me." The very minute you let your guard down, is the opportunity that the crocodile has been waiting for all day.

4

He is victorious who knows when and when not to fight.
Sun Tzu

In Sun Tzu's famous book, *The Art of War*, he makes it clear that it is not always time to fight. You must pick your battles with special care. Granted, sometimes you are faced with a situation that leaves you no other options except for defending yourself on the spot, but these circumstances are few and far between. You have to listen to your spirit and allow your inner voice to guide you. There are no hard and fast rules about when to fight and when not to fight, but it is always wise to only resort to physical action when all other honorable options have been exhausted.

When all other options have been tried and have failed, you still have to know when and when not to strike. Timing can be the difference in victory and defeat. Again, you have to listen to your spirit in order to know when to strike. Opportunities are rare and you must take advantage of them quickly when they arise. When you know in your spirit that it is time to act, don't delay.

If it doesn't feel right inside, it is not right. Remember, sometimes it is necessary to retreat and regroup before you engage. Use common sense in every situation. Don't allow your emotions to dictate your actions. Let your spirit and your intellect show you when and when not to fight. Your spirit will not steer you wrong if you learn to listen to it closely.

5

Don't trouble a quiet snake.
Greek Proverb

Never go looking for trouble. Do your best to live a peaceful life. You will run across a lot of bad guys in your journey through life, but that doesn't mean that you have to confront all of them. It is best to keep your distance from them. Don't associate with them. You can pretty much tell which guys are out looking for trouble instead of looking to have a good time. Avoid them! This is not being a coward or a wimp; it is being smart.

Some guys are just plain dangerous, like a poisonous snake. Sure, if you see a poisonous snake lying coiled on a rock while you are out hiking, you could probably kill it with a stick. But why bother, when it is much easier and safer to avoid it. If you don't confront the snake, there is no chance that you will suffer a deadly bite, and you can both go about your own business. You never know how deadly or how aggressive that snake really is, and it is best not to find out if you don't have to.

The same principle applies to ruffians and street punks. If you are aware, you can pick them out of the crowd. Don't encounter them if you don't have to. Let them go their way and you go your way. It is not necessary to find out how dangerous they may be. Those who play with snakes, even if they are professional herpetologists, many times end up with life-threatening bites. Most times a quiet snake will go his own way, in peace, if he is not challenged. Don't tempt fate.

6

In cases of defense tis best to weigh the enemy more mighty than he seems.
William Shakespeare

Never underestimate your enemy. You really never know just how dangerous or how vicious someone else actually is, and it is always a mistake to see an enemy as no "real" threat. With the weapons available in today's society, there is no enemy that should be taken for granted. Every enemy should be seen as a threat, even if that enemy seems weak and vulnerable.

Your enemy has multiple ways of attacking you in today's world, and the enemies that you may consider weak, will not "play fair." They know inside that they cannot stand up to you man to man. Expect the unexpected. Expect your enemy to be dishonorable and to fight dirty. If you do not underestimate your enemy, you will not allow yourself to become lax in your defense. Don't give your enemies an opening because of your overconfidence.

Overconfidence can be a deadly mistake. Even if you consider your enemy to be weak, watch him like he is mighty. In all honesty, you never really know for sure what someone else is capable of, or the extent of his skills. Many martial arts masters do not look like much of a physical threat, but looks can be deceptive. Don't underestimate any enemy. It is much better to be safe than sorry. Think about this.

7

The bird that offers itself to the net is fair game to the fowler.

Japanese Proverb

The best way to stay away from trouble is to stay away from the places and the situations where you are likely to run into trouble. If you are in a seedy night club full of thugs and people of low character, and you are drinking too much, then you are offering yourself up as fair game. You have put yourself in a bad and potentially dangerous situation. In this situation, you are putting yourself in the hands of people who are not trustworthy or honorable. Depending on how much you drink, you are putting yourself at their mercy. This is not a situation that the warrior should ever find himself in while away from home.

This is only one example of offering yourself up as fair game. There are many others. The point is, as a warrior you should always be aware of your surroundings. You should be in control of your own safety. Wherever you go, the people around you should be safer because you are there. Never compromise your defense. Be smart about the places that you go and the situations that you put yourself into when you are away from home. Stay alert. Stay in control. Be smarter than the fowler who is waiting to catch you in his net.

8

If an art is concealed, it succeeds.
Ovid

Many of the masters tell us not to reveal too much about our abilities. It is smarter if you keep your personal information, your skills, and your knowledge hidden. Don't reveal everything about yourself. Avoid the temptation to "brag" about how talented you are, how you won the last tournament, what a great roundhouse kick you have, etc. You really don't want everyone to know your strengths and weaknesses. This gives your enemies information to use against you and tells them how to prepare to counter your skills if they ever have to encounter you physically.

Now I'm not saying that you can never have conversations about your martial arts, but you should be careful about whom you include in those conversations. Even if you are talking with your close friends, don't reveal everything. You should always keep in mind that today's friends could become tomorrow's enemies, and if they do they will not hesitate to use whatever information that they have filed away against you.

Be smart and play your cards close to your vest. Be even smarter still, and do so without revealing that this is what you are doing. No friend or acquaintance likes to feel as though you don't completely trust him. Consider your actions carefully in order to conceal what needs to be concealed, and at the same time develop relationships with others. The trick is to think before you speak.

9

When irate, clear-minded men never show it then and there. Holding it in, they watch for an opportune moment.
Tiruvalluvar

Stay in control of your emotions. Just because you get angry about something, even very angry, doesn't mean that you need to let everyone know about it. You cannot allow your emotions to control your actions. You have to control both your emotions and your actions. It is a common ploy in battle to try and make someone angry in order to cause him to make a mistake or trap him into doing or saying something stupid. The wise warrior will realize this, control his anger, and make a careful decision about when, or if, to let that anger show, as well as the proper way to express his anger at that time.

Anger can and will confuse your mind if you let it. Instead of focusing on the anger, focus on the situation and what is actually happening. Stay clear-minded and calm, and make a conscious decision concerning the situation and how you should deal with it. There is a time to let your anger out; just make sure that *you*, not your temper, decide when that time will be.

Many people will try to push your buttons purely for entertainment purposes. See their obnoxious attempts to cause you to stumble as nothing more than one more challenge for you on your path to warriorship. Don't let them win. Act as if their rudeness has no effect on you at all. Practice your wit and self-control. When you look at this type of ploy as just part of the game, your anger will be easier to control.

10

An able man shows his spirit by gentle words and resolute actions; he is neither hot nor timid.
Philip Dormer Stanhope

Many people think that when they get angry and explode, it shows that they really mean business. Their belief is something such as, "Boy when I get mad nobody can stop me." This is backwards thinking because when you lose your temper, you are actually less effective and more prone to make mistakes. Your thoughts are not as clear and you do not think rationally. Getting to this point actually shows a lack of discipline and self-control.

The warrior should never lose his temper. On the flip side, he is also not shy about expressing himself when the occasion calls for him to speak up. He should simply state what he has to say and then back up his words with resolute actions. He knows that he doesn't have to get out of control or scream and shout in order to get things done. The warrior simply says what needs to be said, and does what needs to be done, and leaves it at that.

Find the balance between being hot-headed and being timid. The warrior has to maintain equilibrium between these two extremes. No one respects a man who is not in control of his emotions or who often loses control of his emotions. The man who is not in control of his emotions is considered unstable. Gentle words and resolute actions are always the best option.

11

The man of true valor lies between the extremes of cowardice and of rashness.
Miguel de Cervantes

The warrior is neither a coward nor a fool. He is a man of character who evaluates each situation and then takes the appropriate action. If, after careful thought, he decides to engage in battle, it is because he has made a mental decision that he has no other choice. He has weighed his options and made a firm decision that he will then follow through, to the end. His action comes from a place of mental clarity. It is not a rash action, but a calm, rational decision.

Moreover, if he decides that it is not wise to engage in battle at this time, he makes his exit with as much honor as possible. This is not an act of cowardice. His action is not based on fear. It is an act rooted in inner wisdom. He listens to his spirit and follows his inner voice. Although deep inside he would like to engage in this battle and put things right, he realizes that now is not the time and waits for a more opportune moment.

At other times, he simply takes pity on the other person, walks away, and forgets about it, knowing what he could have done had he chosen to take action. Although to others this may seem like an act of cowardice, it is actually an act of honor. The warrior refuses to harm another person if there is any other way out of the predicament. Walking away from an encounter without fighting, no matter how others may perceive it, is a valid and honorable way to end an encounter. Only get physical when all other options have been exhausted.

12

In seeking to save another, beware of drowning yourself.
Sir Francis Osborne

As a warrior, it is your duty to protect those weaker than you and to help those who you have the power to help. Wherever you go, whatever you do, those around you should be safer because you are there. You have been given special training that should enable you to step into the role of "protector" at a moment's notice. You have taken the lifestyle of the warrior seriously and therefore you should take this sacred duty seriously. But there is a difference in protecting others, and being rash and placing yourself in danger.

It is your duty to serve and protect others. It is not your duty to sacrifice your life. Your life is as important as anyone else's life. Your duty is to do what you can to save the drowning person, not to switch places with him. If you have a family to protect and to provide for, you have a higher duty to them than to others. You must make sure that you are safe in order to fulfill your filial duty. Therefore you must do your duty, but do it wisely and rationally.

Although the warrior must be willing to risk his life at times, it is never to be done rashly. Situations do exist in which every warrior must be willing to risk his life, but these times are rare. Don't think that it is a great honor to lose your life for a cause. Think of fulfilling your duty. How can you serve and protect your family and friends if you are no longer around? Think rationally. Be smart.

13

By keeping your weapons in order, your enemy will be subjugated.
Nagarjuna

Nagarjuna tells us that if we keep our weapons in order, our enemies will be controlled. As a modern warrior, you do not walk around carrying weapons, unless you have a specific job that requires that you do so, such as a police officer or a soldier. The weapons of today's warrior are his martial arts skill and his wit. You must keep your weapons in order. This means that you must continue to train, and train seriously.

If your weapons are not kept up, they will deteriorate. You must maintain your weapons and make sure that they are in good working order when and if you ever need to use them. You cannot just obtain a good weapon, learn to use it, put it on a shelf for 10 years and expect to reach for it and use it like an expert when you need it.

Keep your weapons in order It is a continual process to keep your martial arts skills sharp. Don't get lazy. Don't leave your weapons on the shelf to deteriorate and become useless. You may have once been a great marksman, but if you haven't touched your pistol in 15 years, your marksmanship will not be as sharp as it once was. The same principle applies to your martial arts as it does with everything else in your life - use it or lose it.

14

Let us not look back in anger, nor forward in fear, but around us in awareness.
James Thurber

Both anger and fear cloud your judgment and prevent you from making good decisions. These are two emotions that the warrior must learn to conquer and control. You must not let these emotions affect your thought process. Besides these two negative emotions, there are two other things that can negatively affect the mind of the warrior as well: dwelling on the past or the future. The warrior should not waste his energy with either of these.

You cannot live in the past or in the future; you can only live in the present. Being angry about something that happened in the past, or worrying about something that may happen in the future, is a waste of your time and energy. These are both things that you can do nothing about. What you can do is be aware of what needs to be done in this present moment. This moment is where your power lies. Live in the moment. Focus on where you are and deal with circumstances as they are at this present moment.

Dwelling on the past and dreading the future both have a strong connection to anger and fear. Many times thoughts of the past are accompanied by anger. This anger can be directed towards what someone else has done or it can have to do with something that you have done. Either way it is not constructive, just as fearing what may happen in the future is not constructive. Discipline yourself to live in the present moment with peace and awareness.

15

Tolerance and patience should not be read as signs of weakness. They are signs of strength.
The Dalai Lama

Many times people misread the actions of a tolerant and patient person as being cowardly and weak. Tolerance and patience can easily be confused with cowardliness and weakness, because many times they look the same on the outside. What makes the difference in whether a person is acting from a place of tolerance and patience, or acting from a place of fear and weakness, is that person's intentions. Your mind-set is what makes the difference.

Tolerance and patience are characteristics that every warrior should aspire to, and in the true warrior they are definitely signs of strength. They do not come from a mind-set of fear, but from an attitude of discipline and self-control. How do you know whether another person is acting from a position of weakness or strength? You don't, and it is really none of your business. All you need to be concerned with is your own character.

You are in charge of you, nobody else. Make sure your intentions and your attitudes are right. Be willing to walk away in order to resolve a potentially violent situation. This is not being a coward, but is actually an act which takes great strength and self-confidence. Yes, self-confidence. It takes confidence in yourself to walk away when others who are watching may consider you to be a coward. Be confident in who you are and don't worry about the misconceptions of others.

16

Never get angry except on purpose.
Japanese Maxim

No one can "make" you angry. You choose your own emotions. You choose how you will react to each and every situation. Whenever you allow someone or some situation to anger you, without purposely making the decision that it is now time to be angry, you have allowed that person or thing to have power over you. You have given your own power away by not controlling when you will get angry and how you will display your anger.

A warrior must stay in complete control of his emotions. Don't give control of your emotions over to anyone or anything outside yourself. This is part of your training as a warrior; you must learn to control your mind and your emotions. A warrior who is not in control of his emotions is a loose canon. He is a danger to himself and to others. If he allows outside influences to cause him to lose his temper, it is only a matter of time before this character flaw will cause him heartbreak and pain. Trouble always follows the man who doesn't have self-control.

This is not to say that the warrior should never get angry. There is a time and place for the righteous anger of the warrior. The point here is that the warrior himself must purposely decide when it is time to be angry, and exactly how that anger should be expressed. This is a conscious decision that the warrior makes, not an unconscious, immediate reaction. Stay in total control of your mind and emotions.

17

Make benevolence your lifelong duty.
Gichin Funakoshi

Benevolence means kindness, compassion, generosity, and goodwill. These are characteristics that the warrior should strive to obtain. Not only should you strive to obtain these characteristics, but according to Gichin Funakoshi, you should make these "your lifelong duty." That's right, it is your duty as a warrior to be benevolent to others.

Treat others with kindness and compassion. Treat them with respect and be generous with them. Many people that you meet have a hard life and it costs you nothing, and in fact it is your duty, to help them along their path. This is an area that we tend to forget about when we get too wrapped up in our own lives. Don't overlook this important duty.

As a warrior you have been given the gift of special knowledge and training that the majority of people you meet do not have. Do not look down on those who have not had the same opportunities as you. Be kind and compassionate toward them. Know that it is part of your duty to look out for them and to protect them when you can. Remember that benevolence is as much a part of your duty as is any other part of the warrior lifestyle.

18

When the victory is yours, tighten your helmet cords.
Japanese Proverb

We have all seen the movies where the hero has "defeated" the villain at the end of the movie, and just when we think the movie is over, the villain who we thought was defeated, attacks the hero one last time. This happens because the hero "thought" the victory was his and that the fight was over. As he lets down his guard and walks away, he finds out the hard way that he has declared victory too soon, and that he had not finished the job.

Don't quit before the job is finished. When you can see that the victory is yours, do not relax until the battle is over – completely. Too many times people have victory in their hands only to let it slip away because they stop a little too soon. The fire is not out until the last glowing embers have been completely cooled and buried. The battle is not finished until it is over and the enemy is wholly and entirely defeated.

Declaring victory before the battle is 100% finished is a sign of underestimating your enemy. Any time you underestimate your enemy's ability to hurt you, you are taking a great risk. Never underestimate your enemy – any enemy! Make sure the battle is over before you declare victory. Don't let your victory slip away because of your overconfidence.

19

He who fears being conquered is sure of defeat.
Napoleon Bonaparte

I used to attend and participate in martial arts tournaments pretty regularly. One tournament particularly stands out in my mind. I was preparing for a match. As I stretched, the other martial artists were also preparing for the action to begin. I noticed one guy as I was stretching and thought to myself, "I hope I don't get drawn to fight this guy!" He was about 6'5'' and appeared very fit and talented. He was very athletic and muscular, not just tall and lanky.

When it was announced who we would fight in the first match, of course I was drawn to fight this guy. My mind immediately began to run wild and I allowed fear of defeat to enter my mind. In the match, he quickly made a punching bag out of me. Later, as I watched him fight in the other matches, I realized that I could have easily defeated this opponent. His skills were not even close to my own, but I allowed my undisciplined mind to defeat me.

Fear can cloud your mind and interfere with rational thought. Fear can totally psyche you out. You must take control of your mind and not allow fear to cloud your judgment. Focus on what you want to happen, not on what you are afraid might happen. Be confident in your abilities and in your preparations. Think rationally and not emotionally. Know your abilities and have confidence in your skills.

20

There are people in every era who, however adverse the environment, are not corrupted, do not become degenerate.
Masaaki Hatsumi

Today we hear many people blaming the crime rate on poverty. We are told, "It is not the fault of the individual that he committed the crime; it has to do with the extreme poverty that he has had to endure." Well, if this were true, everyone who has had to live in that adverse environment would be committing crimes. But, as we know, everyone who lives in an environment wrought by poverty does not commit crimes. Crime has more to do with individual standards than poverty.

The honor of a true warrior is not situational. By this I mean that you cannot decide to disregard your honor because of your environment. You either have honor or you do not have honor. A man of honor will not set his honor aside when the going gets tough. His honor is not corrupted because the times are rough now. Honor is a permanent part of his being and he will not allow it to become tarnished, no matter how difficult the times have become.

True honor does not degenerate, no matter how adverse the environment. Honor is independent of outside influences. The warrior is the only person who can tarnish his own honor. He is in total control where his honor is concerned. Blaming dishonorable actions on one's personal environment is nothing more than a flimsy excuse which doesn't hold up to those who truly understand the way of the warrior.

21

Strength is defeated by strategy.
Philippine Proverb

Don't always depend solely on your physical skills to protect yourself and those around you. No matter how skilled you are, there is always somebody out there who is stronger, faster and more ruthless. You have to be smart. By all means use the skills you have acquired to protect yourself, but don't forget to also use your head. It is not wise to meet a bigger, stronger, and more skilled enemy head-on.

Use your intelligence and wisdom in order to defeat your enemy. There is no such thing as a fair fight when you are referring to a "real" fight. In a real fight, you use whatever it takes to protect yourself and those you have to defend. One of your weapons is your mind. This should be the first weapon that you employ in any encounter. Keep your mind sharp, just as you keep your other weapons sharp.

Practice the art of not losing control and controlling your emotions. Learn breathing techniques which allow you to stay calm, even in intense situations. No matter how dire the situation is, it only makes matters worse when you lose control and allow fear and stress to control your mind and emotions. Whatever the circumstances you may find yourself in, always keep your mind calm and controlled. Your skills matter little if you panic and fall apart under stress.

22

Think, feel, and act like a warrior.
Set yourself apart from the rest of
society by your personal excellence.
Forrest E. Morgan

Forrest E. Morgan tells us in his book, *Living The Martial Way*, that the warrior is a different kind of person than the ordinary man. He takes his life, his honor, and his duty seriously. He has a real purpose in life. If you want to be a true warrior, you have to think, feel and act differently. You have to go beyond the ordinary. As Forrest Morgan tells us, you have to set yourself apart from the rest of society by your personal excellence in everything that you do.

This is a tall order. It takes discipline and perseverance to live your life this way. Not everyone is able to live the life of a warrior. This lifestyle is a commitment to personal distinction. The warrior knows who he is and what his values are. He sets his own standards and then he lives up to those standards. He is a man of character and strives daily to be worthy of being called a warrior. He lives by a code of excellence.

Living by higher standards than the rest of society is a choice, but for the warrior it is his duty. The warrior has an obligation to himself to strive for excellence in every part of his life. He makes the choice to take life more seriously than his counterparts, knowing deep inside that the reward for living a life of excellence is much greater than any perceived sacrifice. Think, feel, and act like a warrior, and you will become a warrior.

23

Life is a succession of here and now, here and now, unceasing concentration in the here and now.
Taisen Deshimaru

You can do nothing about your past actions. What is done is done and cannot be undone. All you can do is live the best that you can right now in the present moment. You can't change what will happen in the next moment by worrying about what might happen. Worrying and being fearful of the future is only wasting your time in the present. Take care of this moment now, and take care of the next moment when it arrives.

The here and now is all that you really have. There is no such thing as yesterday and tomorrow; they really do not exist. You may have your memories of yesterday, and your hopes for tomorrow, but in reality the only time that you can actually *live* your life is the here and now. Live your life in the here and now. You really have no choice; the only choice that you have is *how* you will live in the here and now.

This is where the warrior has a decision to make. Will you waste your time brooding over how someone has done you wrong or wishing that you had done something differently, or will you move on? Will you spend your time daydreaming about things that you hope for or will you take action and make those dreams come true? The answer for the warrior has to be that he will use his time wisely. The warrior is rational and knows that his time on this earth is short, and that he cannot afford to waste it. Always strive to be present and conscious, and live in the Now.

24

In order to progress in life, one has to improve every day in an endless process.
The Hagakure

There is a term in the Japanese language called kaizen. Kaizen, loosely translated, means constant, never-ending improvement. The warrior must strive daily to improve his life and to live up to the standards that he sets for himself. As Gichin Funakoshi stated in his book, *Karate-Do Kyohan*, "The ultimate aim of the art of karate lies not in victory or defeat, but in the perfection of the character of its participants."

This should also be the ultimate aim of the warrior, to perfect his character. Of course the perfection of character is only one of many goals that the warrior tries to improve on in his daily life, but each of the other goals ultimately lead to this perfection of character that Master Funakoshi spoke of in his teachings. The perfection of your character is the ultimate culmination of all your training.

The warrior has many areas of training that he has to focus on daily. It is his duty to keep his martial arts skills sharp and to train his mind through visualization and meditation. No matter what area he is working on, the warrior strives to improve his skills daily. There is no slacking off. There is no laziness. Make constant, never-ending improvement your goal in life.

25

Avoiding danger is not cowardice.
Philippine Proverb

If you see a group of thugs standing on a street corner and you decide to cross the street and take a different route to your location, you are not being a coward. You are actually doing exactly what you should do. You are using your head, being aware of your surroundings, and taking the necessary steps in order to keep yourself safe. This is not an act of a coward, but an act of a modern warrior.

Sure, you may be able to handle any trouble that may occur if you walk past these thugs, but would that be the smartest strategy? Isn't it a better strategy to avoid danger instead of tempting danger? Not only is this the smarter strategy, but it is also the easiest way to achieve victory over this group in the event that they have less than honorable intentions. You have defeated their strategy without them even knowing what happened. This is the best strategy especially if you have other people with you that you should be protecting.

The warrior doesn't feel the need to prove himself by putting himself in questionable situations. Every violent encounter contains the chance of injury, no matter how skilled you may be. Use your most effective weapon daily - your mind. Be smart and be aware of your surroundings. See danger before you actually encounter it and take steps to protect yourself ahead of time. Avoiding the trap is easier than getting out of the trap.

26

It is no honor for an
eagle to vanquish a dove.
Italian Proverb

As a warrior, you have had special training and know how to defend yourself and others. Not only do you know how to defend yourself, but you know how to render some devastating damage to the human body. With this training comes the responsibility of using that knowledge and those skills conscientiously.

The warrior would not consider it an honor if he defeated a small child in a fight. There is also no honor in using your martial arts skills at the drop of a hat. There is no honor in thrashing some drunk at a bar who has just made some derogatory comments to you. Of course you *could* make him pay severely for his disrespect, but would that be honorable or necessary? Remember, it is an honorable act to walk away from an insult knowing that you have in your power the ability to destroy this person if you so decide, but instead you have decided to be merciful.

Honor requires that the warrior only use his martial arts skills when there is no other option, and then to only use that force which he needs to control the situation. It would not be an honorable act for a warrior to completely annihilate a smaller man which he could easily control without actually injuring him. Not only does this have to do with the warrior's sense of honor, but it is also an important legal consideration. Use common sense and listen to your sense of honor.

27

Noblemen discipline themselves to be dignified at all times... Sharpen your mind and show your dignity.
Matsura Seizen

The warrior should be dignified at all times. This is not to say that you have to walk around somber at all times, never smiling or joking with your friends. You can joke around with your friends and have a good time, while at the same time remaining dignified. There is a big difference in having a good time with your friends and making yourself the buffoon.

We all know the buffoon that I am referring to here. He is the one in the group that always plays the clown and tries to get the laughs. Inevitably, he says inappropriate things, insults people, drinks too much, curses, and in the end, loses the respect of his friends. He makes everyone laugh and continues to be a part of the "group," but deep inside, the other members of the group do not really respect him. He is not dignified and not really respected when push comes to shove.

This should not be the description of the warrior. The warrior should be a man of dignity. He should command respect from his peers, as well as his enemies. Whatever environment he finds himself in, he maintains a sense of who he is and what his values are. He remains dignified, even when he is at ease and relaxed. This is just a natural part of the process of becoming a warrior. The more your standards become ingrained in your spirit, the more natural it becomes for you to show your dignity, no matter what the situation.

28

**Behavior influences consciousness.
Right behavior means right consciousness...
The actions of every instant, every day, must be right...
Every gesture is important.**
Taisen Deshimaru

Everything matters. Everything that you do has a consequence or result. Just as the smallest rock dropped into a still pool of water causes ripples, every action, every word, every thought, causes ripples in the universe. According to Taisen Deshimaru, even every gesture is important. You may not be able to see the results of some of the things that you do, but trust me they are there.

For this reason, it is important for you to strive daily to make your actions, words and thoughts right. You must work daily at perfecting your character. Nobody is perfect in this challenge, but if you continually monitor yourself, you will find that you are getting better and better at controlling your behavior and building your character. Know who you are and what you believe, and then live your code of ethics daily, to the best of your ability.

Behavior influences consciousness, but at the same time, consciousness influences your behavior. It is a never-ending circle. The more you act according to your code of ethics, the more those standards are embedded into your consciousness, and the more your standards are rooted in your consciousness, the easier it is to do the right thing. When you get to this point, doing the right thing becomes a habit; it becomes natural. This is the goal for the warrior.

29

To subdue an enemy without fighting is the greatest of skills.
Sun Tzu

We all train to improve our martial arts skills as warriors. We have confidence that we can defend ourselves and those who depend on us, but we should only use these skills when there is no other option available to us. In Sun Tzu's famous book, *The Art of War,* he tells us that it is a greater skill to subdue the enemy without actually having to resort to fighting. The word "subdue" means to pacify or control. We should try to pacify the enemy. We should try to defuse the situation with words or gestures.

The hard part of pacifying the enemy, for the warrior, is swallowing some of your pride. It takes a lot of discipline and confidence to swallow your pride in order to pacify some rude, aggressive guy who you would rather lay out on the floor. But, as a warrior, it is one of those things which you have to discipline yourself to do. Nobody said that living the warrior lifestyle is easy.

Don't look at these situations like you are letting the other person get the best of you, but rather as a training exercise in the art of war. You are actually controlling the enemy without his even knowing that he is being controlled and manipulated. You are sharpening your arsenal of weapons. Study the art of verbal self-defense and learn how to diffuse potentially dangerous situations without resorting to the use of your martial arts skills. Victories of this kind are even more rewarding than physical conquests.

30

A man who has attained mastery of an art reveals it in his every action.
Samurai Maxim

As this samurai maxim tells us, the man who has attained mastery in the art of warriorship will reveal his mastery in his every action. It is easy to tell the true warrior from the weekend warriors or the want-to-be warriors. The true warrior will act a certain way. There will be a certain energy that surrounds him. You may not be able to put your finger on the reason why, but you will know that there is something special about him.

The warrior's energy seems to put out a special "vibe" that other people can sense. Other people can instinctively tell that this man is not someone to cross. They know that this is a man of honor, a man of his word, a man of character and virtue. They will find the warrior intriguing and interesting, and yet they are not sure why, but they can sense these things through the actions and mannerisms of the warrior. The true warrior can't help it; he will reveal himself through his actions.

The air of self-confidence and dignity that surrounds the warrior is undeniable. His posture reinforces his character. He stands out in the crowd. The warrior doesn't have to blow his own horn in order to be recognized by others. Others recognize his qualities simply by the presence that surrounds him. His mastery of the warrior lifestyle shines through like a beacon in the night.

31

The important thing is to be always moving forward, little by little.
Masutatsu Oyama

Always try to improve yourself every day. Even if it seems like you are not making any progress in your journey to become a warrior, you must continue to move forward. Just as an apple tree does not produce apples overnight, you will not be able to reach perfection as fast as you may like. It is a process and it takes time. The important thing is not to give up and quit, even if it seems like you are not making improvements as fast as you would like.

Improvements come in small increments. Little by little you move forward, sometimes so slowly that you will think that you are not moving at all, but you are. After several weeks or months you will be able to look back at where you started and see the tremendous change that has taken place in your life. Don't stop moving forward, no matter how slowly you seem to be going.

There is an old Chinese proverb which states that one doesn't plant a forest in the morning and cut logs in the afternoon. It takes time for the tree to grow. You must take care of it and keep the weeds from overgrowing it when it is young. The young tree needs water and nutrients in order to mature. The same philosophy can be applied to your progress. You have to be patient and foster the traits and skills that you are trying to develop. Be patient and before you know it, you will find that you have improved in ways which will amaze you. The results will be worth your patience.

32

The true warrior ponders the future without discarding the past while living in the present.
F. J. Chu

While it is true that the present moment is all that we actually have, it doesn't mean that there is no value in the past or that we should not plan for the future. What I mean when I say that you should live in the now, is that you should focus your energy on the present moment; be in the moment. The now is where you live, it is all that really exists, but there is value in the past and you should definitely plan for the future.

You can learn a lot from studying the wisdom and history of the past. The warrior should read and study the wisdom contained in the writings from throughout the ages. Don't discard these writings because of their age. The Code of the Samurai states that the samurai should constantly read the ancient records. This was one way that the samurai maintained their focus on wisdom and integrity. There is much to be learned from the wise men of the past.

It is also important to have goals and plans for the future. Think and plan for the future, but do not worry or become fearful of what may or may not happen. Goals are important for the warrior. The man who does not plan for the future will come to regret it. It is part of the warrior's duty to make sure that his family is cared for, both now and in the future. This is impossible to do without making some preparations for the future. Living in the present moment does not mean neglecting to plan for the future or discarding useful wisdom from the past. Think balance.

33

Trained fighters, much more than average people, have an obligation to employ their skills judiciously. To govern themselves and their emotions at all times.
Peter Hobert

Trained warriors have the ability to be much more dangerous than the average person and therefore have a sacred duty to be careful about the use of their skills. As warriors, we do not have the freedom to let our emotions or tempers run wild. We have to keep ourselves under control at all times. Allowing yourself to lose your temper just once can have devastating and long-lasting consequences.

When you are tempted to let yourself go and lose control, remember the damage that you could do and stop and think about the situation rationally. Is it worth all of the consequences that will come from a minute's loss of self-control? Is the thing that has riled you worth unleashing your wrath? Will you think that this is still important a month from now or a year from now? If not, it probably is not that important now.

Although there will be times when you have to act on the spot without regards to the consequences, the majority of the time you will have time to think before you act. Always remember that our justice system looks at martial artists in a different light than the ordinary man. The courts consider your hands and feet to be deadly weapons, therefore you have to be more careful when it comes to employing your skills than the average Joe. Self-defense means defending yourself from prosecution as well as from bodily harm. Be rational. Be self-controlled.

34

Dignity is not circumstantial.
Kotoda Yahei Toshisada

The dignity of a warrior is not circumstantial. Dignity is synonymous with self-respect and self-esteem. You do not want to put yourself into situations where your self-respect and self-esteem are compromised. Whether you realize it or not, if you lower your standards because of certain circumstances, you also lower your self-esteem. You must maintain your dignity whether you are alone, with friends and family, or with your greatest enemy. You determine your dignity, not your circumstances.

As with honor, you are in total control of your dignity. Nobody can take your dignity from you. Someone may put you in an awkward or embarrassing situation, but how you respond to that situation is totally up to you. No matter what situation or circumstance you have to deal with, you can decide to respond with dignity and honor.

For example, you may be performing a kata during a tournament and for whatever reason, you may slip down and fall flat on your face. Now, you can respond to that embarrassing situation by getting up, cursing, kicking, and just throwing a fit, which would be totally undignified. The other choice, which I hope you would make, would be to get up, continue with your kata to the best of your ability, bow to the judges, and later, be a good sport about the whole thing when your peers start to tease you. This is just one example of responding with dignity, there are many more. The point is dignity is not circumstantial; it is an expected part of the warrior lifestyle

35

You must be deadly serious in training.
Gichin Funakoshi

The above quote taken from *Karate-Do Kyohan by Gichin Funakoshi* pretty much says it all, but how many of us actually pay attention to his admonition? You must take your training seriously, or as Master Funakoshi said, "Deadly serious." He used the words "deadly serious" for a reason. The reason is, if you ever do have to use your skills in a life-or-death situation, your training was "deadly serious" whether you realized it or not. Your attitude and your attention to your training become extremely important at the time that you actually need to put your martial arts skills to use.

It is all too easy to just go through the motions during your training. There are times when you are not in the mood to train and you may be tempted not to workout at all. Remember, the warrior is not practicing martial arts for sport or for some part-time hobby. This is not some game or a fun activity that you participate in twice a week. Your training is about life and death, and you should take your training deadly serious.

If you read the writings of many of the older martial artists, those in their 70's or 80's, they leave no room for doubt that they don't consider practicing martial arts for sport as the true purpose behind the martial arts. Of course there is a place for martial arts competition in today's society, but there is a big difference between sparring for points and the philosophy of "one punch – one kill." The latter is the one in which the warrior should mainly be concerned with perfecting. He knows that when it comes down to the nitty-gritty, there had better be more to his skills than the ability to win a trophy.

36

Focus on your one purpose.
Japanese Maxim

No matter what you are doing, you should focus on your one purpose; put all your attention into whatever you are doing at this very moment. Whether you are practicing your martial arts, studying wisdom from the masters, or gardening, focus on that one thing. There are so many things that vie for your attention today that it is very easy to get sidetracked. It takes discipline to maintain your focus.

There are a multitude of activities that are interesting and good to know something about, but you should always try to have one thing in which you are best. Find your purpose in life. Don't try to be a jack-of-all-trades. Find your one purpose and do your best to perfect that one thing, no matter what that may be.

For the warrior, his purpose is perfecting the skills that he needs to be a warrior. He realizes that being a warrior is his purpose in life. There are many different skills that he has to develop in the process of becoming the best warrior that he can be, but overall his main purpose is warriorship.

Don't try to learn everything about every technique, in every different style of martial arts. You should know a little about the different styles, but make sure you are proficient in your style before learning others. Concentrate and focus. Concentrated energy is much more powerful than energy which is dispersed in different directions. If you want to achieve perfection, focus on your one purpose.

37

This is certain, that a man that studies revenge keeps his wounds green, which otherwise would heal and do well.
Francis Bacon

Revenge is not the way of the warrior. Although there are times when honor demands things be put right, this is a different situation from the act of revenge. Forrest E. Morgan does an excellent job of discussing this distinction in his book, *Living the Martial Way*. I highly recommend that if you haven't read it, you get a copy and read it. It is an excellent book for the warrior.

As for situations where honor does not require action, it is best to walk away from thoughts of revenge. When you dwell on the wrong that someone has done to you, you are only continuing to allow their action to hurt you. It is as if they are getting the best of you over and over again. Don't allow this to happen. Be self-disciplined and control your mind. Get over it and move on with the goals which are important to you.

You will not be able to heal and move on if you are constantly remembering the offense and getting angry about it. Let it go. Focus on your goals. Know that by releasing this incident, you are allowing yourself to continue on your journey towards warriorship without this monkey on your back. Whatever happened, it was not important enough to allow it to interfere with your walk on the warrior path.

38

Though we are powerful and strong, and we know how to fight, we do not wish to fight.

Cherokee Saying

This Cherokee maxim really describes the attitude of the warrior. The warrior is definitely powerful and strong, and he undeniably knows how to fight, but he would be completely satisfied if he went his whole life without ever having to fight. The true warrior does not look for the opportunity to prove his skills in battle. He longs for a peaceful life.

Never go out looking for a fight. This is something that a warrior should never do. In fact, you should do everything in your power, within reason, to avoid having to fight. There are times when you have to make the decision to get physical, but this should only be when all other options have failed and you have no other choice. The decision to fight should be taken very seriously.

There are different forms of doing battle. Remember that your goal is not necessarily to defeat your enemy by getting physical, but to defeat your enemy period. Avoidance, intelligence, and cunning are all alternative ways in which you can totally annihilate your enemy's strategy, and all without the ramifications of a physical confrontation. Just keep in mind that your ultimate goal is to make sure that you are safe, and then to defeat your enemy, by the best means available. The majority of the time, fighting will not be the appropriate choice for the warrior, although this deadly ability is always lying in the background like a tiger in the bush.

39

Opportunity is rare and a wise man will never let it go by him.
Bayard Taylor

A warrior must make the most of every opportunity. This is especially true in a confrontation. If you get the opportunity to use your intelligence to diffuse a situation, you have to grab it immediately. If the situation has deteriorated into a physical confrontation, it is even more important to take advantage of every opportunity. Once the decision to get physical has been made, don't hold back. Use whatever force you need in order to secure your safety.

You may only get one opening during a fight, but for the trained warrior that should be all that is needed. When you see your enemy make his mistake, you must exploit it without delay. Delaying your action could mean defeat. You have to be mentally and physically alert and ready to explode into action the second that the occasion requires you to act.

This takes discipline and courage, as well as good timing. When you have a chance, take it immediately. Strike hard and fast! This is not the time for doubts or second guessing; this is the time for action. There is little time to think at this point. This is what your training is all about. You have to be mentally prepared and know what you should and should not do to keep yourself safe. If you have to slow down and think before you act in this situation, the opportunity may well pass you by before you get a chance to take advantage of it. Trust your training and go on instinct.

40

Never interrupt your enemy when he is making a mistake.

Napoleon Bonaparte

Given enough time, your enemy will make a mistake. Your responsibility is to be patient and allow your enemy the time to slip up. Whether it is a mental lapse, a physical mistake, or a loss of temper, sooner or later your enemy will make a mistake. Many times his mistake will bring about his defeat without much effort on your part.

Be patient and alert. Be ready to take advantage of his every blunder. There is no such thing as fighting fair in a real fight. Take advantage of everything and anything that will help you achieve your victory. Use the weapons that you have available to you at the time. Using the enemy's mistakes is one of the skills that the warrior needs to perfect in order to come out of a physical confrontation on top.

Be patient and let karma work in the lives of your enemies. There is no need for you to take revenge on your enemy. Men who lack honor and integrity will find that sooner or later their mistakes will bring them down. What comes around goes around. Just practice patience and be ready. Your enemy will make a mistake; it is just a matter of when, where, and how severe. When he does make his mistake, strike hard and strike fast. I said that he would make *a* mistake, but I didn't say he would make *multiple* mistakes. You may only get one chance; make it count.

41

He who is an ass and takes himself to be a stag, finds his mistake when he comes to leap the ditch.
Italian Proverb

Don't be overconfident in your skills or abilities. Don't think that you are the toughest man around and nobody else can possibly be a threat to you. There will always be somebody out there who is bigger, stronger, tougher, and more ruthless. I'm not saying that you shouldn't have confidence in your martial arts skills, but make sure that your evaluation of your skills is honest and correct.

You don't want to find yourself in the position of believing that you are a great fighter only to find out in the middle of a violent street encounter that your skills are not quite as sharp as you believed them to be. It is better to discover your weakness in the dojo where you can strengthen your skills in a safe environment, than to discover your weakness in a life-or-death situation. Know your abilities and your limits.

It is very dangerous to have the martial arts skills of Barney Fife, but see yourself as having the martial arts skills of Chuck Norris. Judge your skills rationally and then train to strengthen your weak points. It is no disgrace to have kicks or blocks which are in need of improvement. Everyone has weak spots that could stand some improvement. The shame is having too much pride in yourself to admit that you have some improvements to make, and carrying on a charade to hide your lack of skill. You will never improve your martial arts skills if you cannot realistically evaluate your skill level.

42

The wise hawk conceals his talons.
Japanese Proverb

It is unwise for the warrior to tell everyone about his weapons and his skills. Nothing good comes from bragging. If you actually are skilled in your martial art and you constantly talk about how great you do this or that, sooner or later someone will want to challenge you. They will want to find out how good you really are, and they will be prepared for all of the weapons that you have been bragging about so brazenly. This is just plain not smart.

Then, when you diffuse the situation with words, as you should, you end up looking as if you were lying about your skills, or that you are a coward. If you have been exaggerating your skills, as braggers tend to do, you find yourself in an even worse position. This should never happen to the warrior. It is wiser to avoid talking about yourself or your skills.

Your weapons are no one else's business. Don't give your enemies a "heads up" about your martial arts prowess. That is equivalent to the quarterback announcing to the defense what pass plays he likes to run. Again, not smart. Next time you are tempted to brag or reveal information about your skills, think about why you feel the urge to open your mouth, and then think about the possible consequences. Do you really need someone else to approve of your abilities or pat you on the back in order to feel good about yourself? If you do, you need to do some soul searching and find out why.

43

Take away the cause, and the effect ceases.
Miguel de Cervantes

There is no such thing as luck. Everything happens for a reason. The law of cause and effect is the way of nature. Every action, no matter how small, has a ripple effect. Everything that you do, from the boldest action to the smallest thought, has a consequence that follows along with it. The consequence may be so small and insignificant that you do not notice it, but it is still there. There is a cause for everything. Take away that cause and you take away the effect.

This is why it is so important for the warrior to keep a watchful eye over himself at all times. You must keep this in mind. There is nothing that you can do, nothing that you can say, and nothing that you can think, that will not affect your life in some way. Everything matters. It is important that you live every minute to the best of your abilities. Live according to your code of ethics, whether you are alone or out in public.

If you find that you are constantly dealing with unpleasant consequences, find the cause of those consequences and change it. Change your actions, and you change the consequences. The old saying that it is crazy to continue to do the same things over and over, and expect different results, is true. If you want different results, you have to change what you are doing. If people challenge you and become aggressive every time you go out, you should take a close look at yourself to discover the cause. Take away the cause, and the effect ceases.

44

To be prepared for war is one of the most effective means of preserving peace.
George Washington

No bad guy wants to attack a warrior. The mugger or thug looks for an easy target. These people do not have any honor. They don't want to test their skills against someone who might be able to pound them into the ground. Just like any other predator, they prey on the weak. Therefore, by being in shape and prepared to defend himself, the warrior is actually preventing other people from attacking him. As I said, no one in their right mind wants to tangle with a prepared warrior.

I can already hear some of you saying that this is a contradiction to the Japanese proverb which states, "The wise hawk conceals his talons." But this is not really a contradiction. I'm not saying that you should go around telling everyone how prepared you are as a warrior. You don't have to say anything. Criminals are experts at sensing who they should and should not target. They have a pretty good idea whether or not you are prepared to defend yourself, and those who don't could be in for a rude awakening if you are truly prepared.

George Washington knew that other countries would prey on the United States if they perceived us as weak. When you portray yourself as weak, you are actually doing more to cause violence because predators will be tempted to attack you, but by being prepared for battle, they are deterred. Preserve peace; be prepared for battle.

45

Make yourself a sheep,
and the wolf is ready.
Russian Proverb

There are a lot of bad guys out there and they, as I have said before, are predators. They look for the easy target. Wolves like to attack sheep, not grizzly bears. There is a reason for this; sheep are weak and can't defend themselves, grizzly bears are strong and not only can, but will defend themselves. Sheep are also not the smartest animals on the planet; they tend to wander around aimlessly, making themselves an easy target.

People who have sheep-like characteristics are exactly what the human wolves are looking for in their prey. They wander around aimlessly, oblivious of their surroundings. They tend to not use their brains when they are out and about, either because they are distracted or just too busy. They appear weak and unable or unwilling to defend themselves from any possible attack. When these people leave home, the wolves smell dinner.

In his book, *On Killing*, Lt. Col. Dave Grossman has likened the warrior to the sheepdog. He states that it is their duty to protect the sheep and confront the wolves. He goes on to say that, in general, the sheep do not like the sheepdog, because he looks much like the wolf in that he has "fangs and the capacity for violence." The difference is that the sheepdog would never harm the sheep, but is there for the sheep's protection.

46

**It is foolish to try and live on past experiences.
It is a very dangerous, if not fatal habit,
to judge ourselves to be safe because of
something that we felt or did twenty years ago.**
Charles Spurgeon

Being a warrior is an ongoing lifestyle. It is not a goal in the sense that once you achieve the status of a warrior, you can then relax because you now have all the weapons and training that you could ever need. After all, you have a black belt that you earned, how could anybody ever stand up to you in hand to hand combat? Too many people believe that they are prepared to defend themselves or others because of their past training.

Martial arts training is like paddling your boat up a river; as soon as you stop paddling, you begin to go backwards. If you have ever developed your martial arts skills to a level where you felt you could easily defend yourself, it is hard to imagine that your skills have dissipated and you are no longer at the same level. In your mind you still see yourself as a force to be reckoned with, even if it has been years since you actually practiced your art.

Moreover, many people, even if they were promoted to black belt, were never actually prepared to defend themselves in the first place. Their black belt had more to do with sports and memorization than it did with self-defense. There is also a big difference between a practicing black belt and someone who earned their black belt and then quit working out all together. See things as they are; not doing so can be a very dangerous illusion.

47

The just man is not one who does harm to none, but one whom having the power to harm represses the will.
Pythagoras

The warrior has the power to do severe harm to people who offend him. With all the special training and knowledge that he has, he could easily injure those who cross him. Not everyone has this ability. Everyone doesn't have the power to easily harm others. Furthermore, not everyone who walks away from an insult or a possible fight is doing so out of a sense of justice and self-control.

So what makes the difference in the ordinary man that walks away from an insult, and the warrior that walks away from an insult? Depending on the situation, the ordinary man may not have any choice. He may not be able to stand up for himself. He may be too frightened or weak to address the offense. The warrior has a choice.

I say that the warrior has a choice because just as easily as he walked away from this situation, he could have taken this person's life. The warrior has a choice and chooses to pardon the guy that has just insulted him, knowing that he is doing so, not out of fear or weakness, but from a sense of honor, discipline and self-control. He is a just man. He has the power to do harm, but represses his will.

48

The better part of valor is discretion.
William Shakespeare

Don't rush into every situation trying to be the hero. You have to think rationally about everything that you do. Although the warrior has a duty to serve and protect, he also has a duty to be prudent and to use good judgment. It is foolhardy to jump off a ledge into a pool of water without knowing how deep the pool actually is. Not only is it foolhardy, it could cost you your life.

Be valiant and courageous, but at the same time be cautious. Being cautious is not the same as being a coward or being fearful. It is being smart. Make rational decisions. One wrong decision can have far reaching consequences. There is a time for action and a time for holding back. The warrior must be able to discern the difference between the two and use wisdom in all of his decisions.

Gallantry without discretion is foolhardy. Alexander Pope tells us that fools rush in where angels fear to tread. Action without discretion is characteristic of fools, but it shouldn't be characteristic of the warrior. Making rational decisions concerning heroism and bravery is part of the warrior lifestyle, stupidity is not. Make decisions that will not only add to your honor, but will also keep you and those you love safe. Be smart.

49

He does not guard himself well who is not always on his guard.
French Proverb

A warrior should always be on his guard. This doesn't mean that he has to walk around constantly looking over his shoulder for trouble. It also doesn't mean that he has to be uptight and un-relaxed whenever he is out and about. What it does mean is that he is aware of his surroundings. He is not oblivious to what is going on around him.

When you are leaving the movie or restaurant at night, be aware of your surroundings. Check out who else is around the parking lot when you go out to your car. Just be aware. Also, don't overindulge when you are out on the town. If you have just eaten enough for three men or you happened to drink a little too much, both your awareness and your ability to defend yourself, if the occasion arises, will be compromised.

It is important to maintain your readiness anytime you are away from home. Stay on guard and be ready for the surprises of life. Awareness is the key. Just being aware of your surroundings can keep you safe. Predators are able to take most people by surprise simply because most people are not aware of their surroundings. They wander around with their heads in the clouds and their minds going in 20 different directions. If you are not always alert and aware when you are away from home, you are not guarding yourself as well as you should be to avoid predators.

50

The master warrior is a man of character, a man of wisdom and insight.
Forrest E. Morgan

No man is born with all of the traits in the above quote. These traits have to be developed over time. You have to make a conscious decision to work at acquiring these traits. This means that there is hope for everyone who wants to be a man of character. It is up to you. You make the decision concerning your own character.

So, how do you become a man of character, wisdom and insight? First, you need to make a firm decision about your own standards. Decide what you stand for and what you won't stand for in your life. Then stick to your decision. Study the writings from the men of the past who were men of character, wisdom and insight. Don't just casually read through these texts as you would a newspaper, but actually study what they are trying to teach you. Then put what you have read into action; don't just read it and forget it…live it.

For the true warrior this is not a nice addition to his life. This has to be an integral part of his being. He has no choice about this. He has to be a man of character, wisdom and insight. Martial arts training, without this part of the equation, does not produce a warrior; it produces a dangerous menace to society. Character is the cornerstone for the true warrior. Character is the cornerstone for the true human being.

51

Doing it halfway is no good; you have to do it all the way, give yourself wholly to it.
Taisen Deshimaru

It is easy to get into the habit of thinking about "this, that, and the other thing" when you are in the middle of a workout. This is the result of an undisciplined mind. If you find yourself focusing on other things during your workout, stop yourself and refocus on why you are working out in the first place. Thinking of other things, instead of focusing your energy on your workout, is definitely not taking your training "deadly serious." Your training is too important to do half-heartedly. Focus all your energy on the task at hand.

Arnold Schwarzenegger pointed out during his bodybuilding years that your muscles actually increase in size and get bigger if you concentrate and visualize this happening as you workout. Now, if concentrating on your weight training increases the effectiveness of your workout, why wouldn't the same be true concerning your martial arts workout? What you concentrate on matters. Our mind has much greater powers than we give it credit for having.

Do you want to increase your flexibility? Visualize your muscles lengthening and becoming more flexible and stronger as you stretch. If you want to make your front kick stronger, visualize yourself going through each part of the kick. Focus totally on your kick when you are practicing it. If you are not including your mind in your workout, you are leaving out a vital part of your training. Don't workout half way, give yourself wholly to your training.

52

When you step beyond your own gate, you face a million enemies.
Gichin Funakoshi

Every time you leave your home and venture out into the world you should be aware of your surroundings. Be aware that there are bad guys out there. You may or may not recognize them as your paths cross, but they are there. As a warrior, you should recognize this fact and not walk around in a daze when you are in public. Many times it seems as if people walk around in a semi-hypnotic state, unaware of their surroundings or the people around them. This is unwise and dangerous.

Discipline your mind. Stay aware of both your surroundings and what is going on wherever you may find yourself. This doesn't mean that you should see everyone as your enemy when you leave home, but you should realize that many of the people that you see are not going to be upstanding people of good character. Be careful and aware when you are outside of the security of your own gate.

Learn to recognize the character traits of the predator and be aware of anyone who displays these traits. Also, realize that predators are very skilled at disguising these traits. Not everyone who displays the behavior of a predator is going to be a threat to you, but it is always best to play it safe. The key is always being aware of your surroundings. Keep this little piece of wisdom from Master Funakoshi in the back of your mind whenever you leave home, as a reminder to be alert and attentive.

53

But here we may wonder what he would do if nobody knew anything about it.
The Code of the Samurai

What would you do if you knew that there was absolutely no possibility that anyone else would ever find out about your actions? According to *The Code of the Samurai by Thomas Cleary*, this is a question that every warrior should ask himself. Would this fact change the way that you think about things or would you continue to live by the standards that you have set for yourself? This question is the true test of your character.

The real warrior would live the same way and adhere to the same high standards whether anybody else knew about his actions or not. Even if all laws were abolished and we had a world of complete anarchy, his standards would not change. To men of character, their standards are not flexible. Their honor is not negotiable. Whether they are alone or in the middle of thousands of people, their character is set in stone.

To the samurai, this question was an insinuation of hypocrisy. If a man is sincere about his beliefs and his code of ethics, he doesn't just live by them on some occasions, while at other times completely ignoring them. He lives the life of the warrior seven days a week, regardless of who is watching. Keep a check on your character. Ask yourself, "What would I do if nobody else knew about it?"

54

The angry man will defeat himself in battle as in life.
Samurai Maxim

If you will pay attention as you go through life, you will see many people who allow their anger to defeat them. They will get angry and say or do the wrong thing. I have seen anger cost people jobs, friendships, money...the list could go on and on. Don't be defeated by your anger. Don't give your enemy an easy victory. An angry mind is never a conscious, rational mind.

I have seen many fighters at tournaments that have fought well until they lost their composure. It is fairly easy to tell when a fighter has lost his composure and has given in to his anger. His punches, instead of being controlled and focused, become wild and erratic. His kicks also become sloppy and frequently miss his targets, while at the same time leaving him open to his opponent's counter attacks. It is obvious from his behavior that he has lost his poise and is trying to inflict a painful blow just as much as he is trying to score points.

I have rarely seen someone win a match, who has allowed his anger to take control of his thinking and his actions. More often, the person who loses his cool loses the match, along with a portion of his dignity and respect. It is self-deception to believe that you are unstoppable when you get really angry. I believe that if you think back to the times in your life when you have allowed your anger to control your actions, you will find that your anger did not win you any victories. On the contrary, the angry man usually ends up defeating himself.

55

Peace is not the lack of war, but an inner virtue which has its source in the courage of the soul.
Baruch Spinoza

The word "peace" has several meanings. It does mean freedom from war, but for the warrior, a better definition is "mental calm." Peace is a state of mental calm and serenity, with no anxiety. It is a state of harmony. You can have a feeling of peace no matter what situation you find yourself in. But it takes self-discipline and constant thought control. Just as you train your body to react in certain ways, you have to train your mind to be peaceful.

Much of this book has been concerned with having a disciplined mind. The mind plays such a huge part in the life of the warrior. I have said several times that you have to have a disciplined mind, but how do you discipline your mind? The best way to discipline your mind is through meditation. Learn to meditate. A calm warrior is a mindful warrior, and a mindful warrior is a rational warrior.

The art of meditation is simple, but it does take practice to perfect. Start slow and learn to quiet your mind for several minutes. This is harder than it sounds. Thoughts will continue to disturb the silence, but with practice you will soon find that you can quiet your mind for longer periods of time. The practice of meditation is essential to your quest for warriorship.

56

Do not seek to follow in the footsteps of wise men, seek what they sought.
Basho

Too many people idolize the martial artists or great philosophers of the past. They put them on pedestals almost like they were gods. They want to be like them; they are almost obsessed with them. You shouldn't focus so much on the person, but on what that person tried to teach. What was it that these masters sought and what did they want to teach others? What thoughts did these wise men have and why?

Warriors do not try to imitate someone else. They shouldn't try to be exactly like Bruce Lee or Lao Tzu. What they should do is seek the perfection that the great men of the past sought. Seek the perfection of your martial arts skills. Seek the perfection of your character. Seek wisdom, discipline, knowledge, and honor. Dedicate yourself to seeking what they sought, not to the man himself or any specific philosophy. Men are just men, no matter how great they were; seek the Source. Seek what they sought.

If we were able to actually sit down and engage in a conversation with the great teachers of the past, I believe that they would tell us this exact same thing. They would say, "I am nothing special. You should seek wisdom and knowledge. Do not seek to be my disciple." Great teachers will teach their students how to think, not what to think. It is with this knowledge that we should read the wisdom of the elders.

57

Anger breeds confusion. To be clear-minded you must avoid being angry.
The Bhagavad Gita

You must control anger to be clear-minded. Giving vent to your anger may give you some temporary satisfaction, but in the end, after you have calmed down, you will see that it has interfered with your rational thinking process. Anger causes your mind to be confused. You don't think straight when you are angry. Science has now proven that, not only does anger cloud your thinking process, but extreme anger or stress actually kills brain cells. Trying to deal with a stressful situation, while at the same time you are killing your brain cells, doesn't seem like a wise decision to me. What do you think?

Everyone gets angry. That is just part of being human. The trick is to be able to successfully control your anger and not let your anger cloud your thinking and cause you to make mistakes. It is not the anger that is the problem; it is the lack of self-control. You must be able to control your emotions, to get past the anger and still function rationally.

There are many ways to deal with anger. Find one that works for you and train yourself to manage your anger. One way to successfully deal with your anger is to change your perception concerning the thing that has annoyed you. If you change the way that you look at the issue at hand, your emotions towards that issue will change also. Remember, you can't afford to allow outside pressures to influence your thought process. No matter what is happening in your external environment, keep your mind calm and rational.

58

The hunter can make many mistakes, the hunted, only one.
Native American Maxim

Most criminals are predators. They "hunt" for the weak, the unaware, and the unprepared. They can afford to make some mistakes and still survive to "hunt" another day. It may take several "hunts" for the criminal to bag his prey, but he learns from his mistakes and continues to hunt, perfecting his skills as a predator.

The "hunted" on the other hand, cannot afford to make a mistake. He may not get a chance to learn from his mistake. The "hunted" has to remain alert at all times, being aware of his surroundings, constantly watching for the predators who seek to prey on him. One mistake may cost him his life.

This fact actually makes it more important for the warrior to have sharp self-defense skills. You don't have the luxury of learning from your mistakes on the streets. Those mistakes could be a permanent lesson. The warrior has to be ready for the attack. Even if the predator makes a mistake and fails in his quest, he can still do some serious damage to his prey, if his prey is unprepared.

The warrior has to be alert and aware of his surroundings at all times. He cannot afford to let down his guard. Why does the warrior need to be alert and aware at all times? The Native American maxim above summarizes the answer to this question perfectly. Think about it.

59

Your reality check must be done long before you actually find yourself confronted with a life and death, kill-or-be-killed situation.

Dirk Skinner

It is very important for the warrior to judge his skills and readiness to deal with a violent conflict honestly and accurately. You need to know ahead of time how much force you are willing to use and in what circumstances you are prepared to use that force. You have to decide how far you will go in defending yourself and those who depend on you. Are you mentally prepared, as well as physically prepared, to do what it takes in an actual self-defense situation?

Being mentally prepared for a confrontation is just as important as being physically prepared. All the training in the world will do you no good if your mind panics in a life-or-death situation. For the warrior, being prepared means that he is prepared in every area of his life - spiritually, mentally, and physically. Train your mind as well as your body. Know what you are prepared to do and what you are not prepared to do, before the occasion arises.

This is where your visualization practice can come into play. Visualize different attacks in different circumstances, with different people, and then see yourself responding to each one in the way which you feel is right. This practice will establish your response in your mind. Essentially, it is like you have already experienced this attack, although it was only in your mind. This is part of your mental training, a very important part.

60

The body and soul of a tactician must always be prepared for battle. If one is unprepared, one is certainly on the way to defeat.
Kazumi Tabata

The warrior has to always be prepared. You never know what kind of situation you will find yourself in when you leave your home. Nobody plans on being mugged or attacked when they go out for the night, but it happens all the time. The one time that you go out and drink too much, or you are unprepared in some other way, could be the one time that you will actually need your skills to be their sharpest.

If you decide that tonight you are just going to relax and party without any concerns, then you are placing your safety in the hands of chance. You are just banking on the odds that nothing bad will actually happen and that you will not have to use your skills. The warrior shouldn't leave his safety to chance. He should maintain control and should always be prepared to meet whatever comes at him. Don't gamble on the odds that the bad guys will be taking the night off.

There is a big difference between investing your money by putting it into a slot machine and investing your money in a wise investment after studying the market. The first is relying on chance. It is the lazy man's way, and more often than not, it leads to losing your money. Don't rely on luck or chance; rely on your own preparations. Stack the odds in your favor. Be prepared.

61

A fool gives full vent to his anger, but a wise man keeps himself under control.
The Book of Proverbs

Have you ever noticed that when most people get angry, they actually look and sound foolish? They say stupid things and make ridiculous threats and statements that they neither mean, nor could back up if they did mean them. After everything has calmed down, people usually have lost respect for the person that has lost his temper. He is thought of as a fool or a ridiculous man with no self-control.

Compare the action of the man who loses his temper with the man who remains in control of his emotions. The man who keeps his cool is usually looked upon with more respect after the incident. Everyone knows that he could have lost his temper, and maybe he had a perfect right to lose his temper, but he chose self-control instead. This man is seen as wise and is looked up to after the incident is over.

There is a great distinction between the two descriptions above. One of the obvious differences is that one man loses respect after the incident and the other man has gained respect after the incident. As a warrior, you must not do anything which will cause you to lose respect. All your actions must be carefully considered and calculated. The warrior should not be seen as a fool, but as a wise man that has total control of himself at all times. Which man do you want people to associate you with?

62

Fear makes the wolf bigger than he is.
German Proverb

When my oldest son was young, he was fighting in a martial arts tournament in New Mexico. There was another boy in the tournament that had already had several fights during the tournament and it was obvious that he and Stephen would be facing each other in the final round. This kid had a great kick and had used it to score points over and over on every boy that he had fought that day.

I could see fear starting to enter into Stephen's mind as he watched this boy destroy one competitor after another. I took him aside and discussed this with him, calmed him down, and eventually he went on to win the match. He took control over his fear and started to think rationally. Had he entered the match with his mind fearing the other boy's kick, things would have probably come out differently.

The warrior must control his fear. Fear can defeat you. It can cloud your judgment and affect your mind in other negative ways. You cannot allow the emotion of fear to control your mind. Anxiety and worry have no place in the life of the warrior. The warrior should think rationally about every situation and then decide the best course of action. When he has done the best that he can do, he has done his duty; he has done all there is to do.

63

Gratitude is the sign of noble souls.
Aesop

Character is one of the traits of the true warrior. In fact, character is one of the most important traits of the warrior. Without character, there is really no warrior, but rather just a person who should have never been given the gift of martial arts training. Character is vital to warriorship.

Gratitude is an important part of good moral character, and the warrior never takes gratitude lightly. When someone does a favor for you, no matter how large or how small, you are indebted to that person until you have repaid that favor. The Japanese have a term for this; it is called giri. Giri is your duty to repay your debts. You should not just say thank you and then forget about it. This is not the way of the warrior. You have incurred a debt and not paying that debt is an act of dishonor.

It doesn't matter if it is a small favor or something much more important, a debt is a debt, and the warrior is honor bound to return the favor. Hold yourself to a higher standard than the average person. Live by your own set of standards, standards that require gratitude and appreciation to be shown when someone else helps you in any way. Be a noble soul. Never fail to express your gratitude, even for the smallest things.

64

There can be no greater virtue
than to hold honor dear.
Men who do will fear no danger
nor commit any unseemly act.
Francesco Guicciardini

Honor is extremely important to the warrior. You will never have to worry about a man of honor cheating you, robbing you, lying to get an advantage, etc. His honor will not allow him to commit such acts. He holds himself to a higher standard, one which forbids him from such low actions. The warrior's actions define him.

The warrior is a man of honor. He sets his own standards and those standards are more stringent than the laws of the land. The warrior has his own set of rules and will not break them or excuse himself from abiding by them. He does not lie, cheat, or steal to gain a personal advantage over his fellow man for personal gain. He is a man that you can rely on to keep his word and to back up what he says. Honor, character, and integrity are dear to him.

Many of my students ask me why they shouldn't cheat in school when it seems that so many of their friends cheat with no consequences. The answer is that there are always consequences. The students who are cheating may not be experiencing consequences from the school, but they are dishonoring themselves. They are proving that they have a severe flaw in their character. Where is their honor? This goes back to the question of what would you do if you knew you wouldn't get caught. Do you want to be a person who only does the right thing when others are looking or do you want to be a warrior?

65

Malice sucks up the greater part of its own venom, and poisons itself.
Michel Montaigne

Malice is the intention or desire to cause harm or pain to someone else, usually because of feelings of revenge. Michel Montaigne tells us that malice is actually poisonous and that the person who holds these negative feelings towards others is actually poisoning himself. While it is true that actually following through on these thoughts of revenge will inflict pain on the other person, your actions will not leave you unscarred.

What man in his right mind would poison himself? Your answer may be that a man in his right mind would never do such a thing. But according to Montaigne, that is exactly what you are doing if you harbor these kinds of thoughts towards others. The path of the warrior is hard enough without continually poisoning yourself through negative thoughts of malice and revenge.

Some people seem more inclined to harbor thoughts of revenge than others. If you are one of the people who have a hard time getting over a wrong which has been done to you, this is a chink in your armor that has to be addressed. Remember, the warrior doesn't just ignore his weak points, but instead he works to strengthen them until they are no longer a liability. Get rid of malice and thoughts of revenge in your life. Keep your thoughts focused on your goals and you will not have time for thoughts of malice.

66

To respond immediately to an angry person is like throwing fuel on a fire.
Spanish Proverb

The true warrior should become an expert at handling an angry man. Most times in a conflict, the angry man can be calmed down and the situation can be handled without things getting physical. Angry people will usually calm down pretty quickly if they are handled correctly. Never respond to an angry person with a fiery comeback, even if he deserves it. This will only increase his anger. As the proverb above states, this only adds fuel to his fire.

Instead, remain composed and try to calm his anger. You already know that you have him defeated, because he has allowed anger to get the best of him. This is a perfect time to practice the skill of defeating your enemy without fighting. Don't allow his anger to become your anger. If you can't control this situation without things becoming physical, use his anger against him to defeat him physically. Either way, his anger has defeated him.

You may fight fire with fire, but you don't fight anger with anger. In fact you shouldn't fight at all if you are angry. Allow the angry man time to catch his breath and think. Most people will calm down after they have had time to think about things. Don't respond immediately if you can avoid it. If you have to respond immediately, respond with a soft, but dignified reply. Remember, your goal is to defeat your enemy, not to appear as though you got the best of him verbally. Think about this.

67

Though your enemy seems like a mouse, watch him like a lion.
Italian Proverb

There are no insignificant enemies, especially today. There are so many ways to hurt someone in today's culture that any and every enemy has to be watched like he is as dangerous as a lion. There are many books on the market that teach people how to get revenge on other people or how to damage them personally.

The enemies of today's warrior usually do not have the courage to face the warrior man to man. Men of honor will not be at odds with the warrior, so he will usually find himself at odds with men of low character. His enemies are usually cowards and men of the worst kind, with no morals and even less honor.

These people are the types that try to hurt people behind their back. They fight with lies and propaganda, or get other people to fight for them. Enemies like these hide behind their manipulation of the law or of their wealth. They can be much more dangerous than the average thug in the street for the warrior. A thug is easily handled by the well-trained warrior; the cowardly, mouse-like enemy, on the other hand, is conniving and scheming. Watch him like a hawk.

68

Trust in today's friends as if they might be tomorrow's enemies.
Baltasar Gracian

Never put too much trust in your friends or acquaintances. No matter how good a friend you think you have, you should not trust them with enough information that they will have the ability to use it against you in some way. Today's best friend can turn against you faster than you can imagine. People that you think will never ever turn on you, could be your worst enemy tomorrow.

You can still have good friends without arming them with information concerning your private affairs. No matter how good of a friend you think you have, not everything should be discussed with him. If they turn out to be your tried and true friend, great, if not, then you have avoided arming them with any weapons that could be used against you. The bottom line is that you should always watch what you say. Don't say too much. Keep personal and private information to yourself.

Not everything is other people's business. Don't feel the need to share every single thing about your life with others. Some people feel the need for the approval of others to confirm that they are on the right path. The warrior should know he is on the right path independent of whether or not others approve of his lifestyle. He doesn't need their stamp of approval to live by the standards that he has set for himself. Have confidence in yourself.

69

By associating with good and evil people a man acquires the virtues and vices which they possess, even as the wind blowing over different places takes along good and bad odors.
The Panchatantra

The choice of who you will associate with is a very important decision. No matter how strong your character is, if you associate with people of low moral fiber, it will be hard to maintain your character. You will naturally begin to acquire some of their bad traits. It may be a very subtle process, but it will happen nonetheless. This is just a law of nature.

If you associate with people of good character, you will start to become more like them. If you associate with people of low character, you will start to become more like those people. Since perfecting your character should be one of your main goals as a warrior, associating with people of low character is actually hindering the achievement of your goals.

Make a decision to only associate with quality people that will help you achieve the goals that you have set for yourself. Associate with men of honor. Sure, you will have to do business with all kinds of people, but this doesn't mean that you have to develop close relationships with them. Close friendships should be reserved for men of honor, not every person that you meet. In fact, there is no true friendship between people of low character. They are not people that you can count on when your back is against the wall.

70

There are nine hundred and ninety-nine patrons of virtue to one virtuous man.
Henry David Thoreau

There are a lot of people who will talk the talk, but not walk the walk. Many people will refer to their honor, but at the same time will lie, cheat and steal if money is involved. Sure, they will have their reasons and will justify their actions, but you can't take "real" honor on and off like your jacket. Either you are a man of honor, or you are not a man of honor. You can't have it both ways.

Don't be one of those people who talk about honor and character, but in the end really can't live up to what they profess. Living a life of honor is not always an easy path to walk. Men of honor put their honor before their comfort or their convenience. People who are talkers but not doers, put their comfort and convenience first and squeeze honor in when it is convenient for them to do so.

The warrior should be a man of honor and virtue. He should walk the walk, and leave the talk to others. When Thoreau strongly disagreed with the government, he refused to pay his taxes. Because of his stand, he was threatened with jail, but still he refused to go against his conscious and pay his taxes.

He stated that it was against his conscious to support a government whose policies he considered immoral. As a result, he was arrested and did spend time in jail. Thoreau lived his standards, no matter what the consequences. This should be the warrior's attitude toward his code of ethics - uncompromising resolve.

71

If you are not sure, don't act.
Bodhidharma

To be sure whether or not your actions are right, you have to spend time listening to your spirit. Don't be rash. Deliberate long and hard before getting involved in other people's affairs. When you aren't sure what to do, it is wise to do nothing until you are sure.

It is a common sales tactic to try and get someone to make a quick decision. They want you to buy now, because they know if you take the time to think about it you will see through their sales gimmicks. The salesman doesn't want you to think things through. He wants you to act on impulse.

Don't be rushed into making important decisions. When you aren't sure what to do, do nothing; just wait. Get your mind off the issue at hand. Do something else that has absolutely nothing to do with the decision that you are trying to make. This allows your mind to clear away the fog surrounding the issue so you can think clearly.

Meditate on the issue, and the information that you have been given, and your spirit will help you determine what you should do. If you don't feel right about it inside, it is probably not right. When you know what the right course of action is, act. Until you *know* what you should do, do nothing. Don't be rash; be rational.

72

It is not only what we do,
but what we do not do,
for which we are accountable.
Moliere

You are accountable for both your actions and your lack of action. As a warrior you are expected to do the right thing; you are expected to make your decisions in accordance with your honor. There are times when you can do wrong by taking no action at all. For example, if you see a lady being harassed by two thugs, and you decide to do nothing and walk on by, you are accountable for your lack of action. You are a warrior and you have the duty to get involved and protect this lady. Your lack of action would be against your code of honor.

A warrior has a greater duty than the average man. He has a responsibility to protect the weak and those in need. Not doing so, when he has the opportunity, is a dishonorable act. If you see an injustice and take no action, is that a sign of courage or cowardice? How do you think the "real" warrior would react in this circumstance? Take action when action is needed. Don't let fear or indecision cause you to simply do nothing when duty is screaming for you to act. Live the code that you profess. Be able to rationally explain both your actions and your inactions.

73

To see what is right and not to do it is cowardice.
Confucius

Sometimes taking the right course of action seems as though it will cost you dearly, but the true warrior will put what is right over what is profitable. Your duty as a warrior is to do what is right, not to worry about the consequences of doing the right thing. Honor requires that if you know what you should do, you do it. Doing the right thing takes courage. It takes fortitude, especially when the majority is against you.

Doing the right thing is a trait of the warrior. There have been many examples throughout history where an army or a group of men have been outnumbered to the point where they had virtually no chance of survival if they decided to stand up and fight. Staring death in the face, they still made the decision to stand and fight. They chose to stand for what they felt to be right, at all costs. To them, doing otherwise would have been cowardly and that was not an option.

This is the type of conviction that the warrior should have concerning doing what is right. Once he has decided what is right in a certain situation, he should stand on the side of what is right at all costs. Yes, this does take a lot of courage and fortitude. It takes self-confidence and integrity beyond the average man. In short, it takes a true warrior.

74

A man's word is his honor.
Okinawan Proverb

Your word is your honor. In today's world there doesn't seem to be many people who think this way. People will say whatever gets them what they want, whether it is true or false, right or wrong. Most people don't seem to care about their "word," but then again, most people do not have a clue what true honor is either. You should think before you speak and you should honor what you say.

Honor consists of multiple parts. It is a complex idea in which intention plays a huge role. Think about the intentions behind your words and your actions. What is the purpose behind your words? Do your words even have a purpose? *The Code of the Samurai* tells us that the warrior should carefully consider every word that comes out of his mouth. Be conscious of your words.

As a warrior, your word should be as binding to you as any written contract. If you say that you will do something, do it, period. If you make a promise, you have a debt to fulfill. Those who take honor seriously will always honor their word, and warriors take honor seriously. Make your word your bond. Make your word your honor. Say what you mean and mean what you say.

75

Don't appear just; be just.
Aechylus

It is part of your duty to build your character and to be just. Many people in this world appear just, but behind the veil they are really people of low character. They will lie and cheat, and will do virtually anything to get what they want. We constantly see politicians who fit this image. They talk about their good character and honor. They seem like upstanding men and women. Then one day, when the scandal breaks, we find out the truth about these people. Their character was just a charade.

Don't be an actor. Don't pretend to be something that you aren't, especially in the area of your character. You should not have the appearance of being a man of character and virtue in public, but in private live a different way. Don't fake character; build character from the inside out.

Nobody respects a hypocrite, nor should they. La Rochefoucauld taught that hypocrisy is the tribute that vice pays to virtue. This means that people can see the value of being a just man, but they aren't willing to make the sacrifices that it takes to truly obtain this character trait. If they couldn't see the value in being just, they wouldn't pretend to have this quality. Take the duty of perfecting your character seriously. Be a man of real honor, not counterfeit honor. Don't appear just; be just.

76

The silent person is often worth listening to.
Japanese Proverb

Throughout history the sages have told us that men of wisdom are also men of few words and that men who talk a lot are men whose wisdom is questionable. People who talk a lot probably are not people who give much thought to their words. You can be fairly sure that men of few words usually think before they speak.

Although quiet men do not talk a lot, their minds are usually engaged and they are thinking about what is being said in the conversation. For this reason, it is very often worth listening to the silent man when he does speak. When the silent man speaks, he usually has something important to say. He does not speak just to hear himself talk or because he wants to "put in his two cents worth."

If he has nothing important to say, he usually says very little. Don't babble. When you have something to say, say it, but don't talk just to break the silence. Be a man whose words mean something. Spend more time listening and observing, than you do chattering away. You learn much more by sitting silently and listening to others talk, than you do by trying to show others how much you know. Cultivate the reputation of being a man worth listening to – a man of wisdom.

77

**You cannot talk to a frog in a well about
the vast sea; he is limited to his area of space.
A summer insect has no knowledge of snow;
it knows nothing beyond its own season.**
Chiu Shu

You will find that the majority of people out there will not be able to understand much of the warrior lifestyle or why you would chose to live this lifestyle. This is becoming even more evident as the moral character of our world seems to continue to degenerate. People just can't understand why you would risk your life to defend a stranger or why you won't lower your standards just for the time being or just until the deal is done.

People who do not take honor seriously cannot comprehend why anyone would put their character and honor ahead of their comfort or finances. It just does not compute for them. They think that this is ridiculous. These people have no concept of true honor and therefore can't understand the warrior lifestyle. Talking to them about the standards of a warrior is about as productive as talking to them about quantum physics.

Be selective with whom you share this information. Understand that not everyone will be sympathetic to your quest. There are but few who are able to understand the way of the warrior, and fewer still, who are able to live by the warrior ideals. Just as a summer insect cannot understand the concept of snow, they cannot comprehend the warrior lifestyle.

78

How often do we supply our enemies with the means of our own destruction.
Aesop

Have you ever noticed how many times on reality television shows people get into hot water because they say too much? They tend to hand their competition exactly what they need to defeat them in the game. I see it over and over; people just can't seem to keep their mouths shut. They begin to talk without thinking and their enemies take advantage of it. It never fails.

You should not reveal any more personal information than is absolutely necessary. The more information that you give someone about yourself, the higher the chances are that you will give them something that they can use against you somewhere down the line. And make no mistake about it, your enemies will make note of every little thing that they can possibly use to defeat you or hurt you.

Small things mentioned in casual conversations can be turned around and used against you if you aren't careful. Don't supply your enemy with the weapons that he needs to destroy you. Be discreet in your conversations, but do so without appearing too secretive. Nobody likes to feel like something is being kept from them, especially your friends. Although it is important that you keep some things private, it is just as important as to how you go about doing so. This is a balancing act that requires you to actually think before you speak.

.

79

We make war that we may live in peace.
Aristotle

We hear a lot of people today say there is never any reason to resort to violence. This is a nice, idealistic view of the world. It would be great if everyone was a peace-loving, rational human being. The warrior would very much love to be a part of a world where everyone could be trusted to have everyone else's best interest in mind. He would relish a world where everyone was a rational human being of high moral character. This would be a peaceful, perfect world. By nature, the true warrior is a peace-loving person.

But, the warrior does not have the luxury of being able to view our current world in these terms, mainly because this is not a realistic view of the world in which we live. In reality, there are evil people out there and these people do not have anyone's interest in mind besides their own. They are not peaceful and do not have high moral character. They are predators who love to hear people say that "there is never any reason to resort to violence." To them this is just an announcement that this person will not resist any attack; this person is easy prey.

The warrior knows that there are reasons to resort to violence. He doesn't expect bad people to refrain from doing bad things. He sees things as they really are, not as he wishes they were. In the end, someone has to be ready to deal with the predators of this world. That someone is the warrior.

80

Carelessness is a great enemy.
Japanese Proverb

Carelessness can defeat even the most skilled warrior. No matter how great your skills are, if you get careless or overconfident you can find yourself in trouble. Pay attention to even the smallest details. Don't take anything for granted. Everything matters. For the prepared warrior, it is carelessness in the small details which can get him in trouble. Stay alert and stay focused.

I once found myself in a physical confrontation where I discovered the truth contained in this proverb firsthand. Although I tried every possible thing that I could have done to stop this encounter from getting physical, this guy's mind was set on using my face as a punching bag. Drugs played a major part in his decision, as they often do with violent trouble makers. He insisted on attacking me. I'm sure that he felt confident in the fact that he could thrash me since he was at least six inches taller than me.

After a short struggle, I was able to end the encounter with one punch, but carelessly my punch was just off target. My careless punch, although it ended the fight, left me with a broken hand. The punch was only off by an inch, but carelessness in even the smallest details can cost you big time. That one little mistake cost me months of pain and some major lost training time, not to mention the doctor bills. Carelessness is one of your worst enemies and an enemy which must be defeated.

81

To spare the ravening leopard is an act of injustice to the sheep.
Persian Proverb

As a teacher I have had to deal with several menacing students over the years. I had one student who was constantly disruptive, threatening and abusive to both teachers and students. Other students were afraid of him. He disrupted the education of students who actually wanted to learn and make something of their lives. This student made threats to teachers and students alike.

With all of this going on for months, the administration refused to expel this student because they wanted to be "compassionate." The other side of the coin is that their compassion for this student was actually an act of injustice to all of the other students and teachers. The same thing goes for our justice system. When our justice system has mercy on the violent criminal and gives him a light sentence or probation, it is really an injustice to the next person this criminal assaults.

Warriors are by nature compassionate people, but there are limits to their compassion. When a wolf is killing your sheep, is it your duty to be compassionate to the wolf or to the sheep? A decision has to be made. Do you spare the wolf or protect the sheep? You can't do both. The warrior should always stand on the side of justice.

82

The best armor is to keep out of range.
Italian Proverb

The best self-defense tactic is to stay away from places where trouble is likely to happen. If you are careful about where you go and when you go there, you may live your whole life without ever having to call on your self-defense skills in a real-life situation. Don't hang out where the thugs and trouble makers prefer to congregate. Associate with people of character. As a rule, you usually do not find people of character and thugs in the same place.

Years ago I found myself at a party that could be classified as one of those places where the thugs hung out. I found that there were several people at this party who seemed to have an extreme dislike for me. Out of the blue, I found myself being grabbed from behind and a folding razor blade being held to my throat. Now, once you get yourself in that kind of position, you are at your enemy's mercy; this is not a good position to be in to say the least.

The point here is that if I had been at the movie theater instead of this party filled with thugs, my safety would have been assured, or at least in my own hands instead of depending on the mercy of a thug who was too high to be rational. My lack of judgment led to my being within a ¼ inch of the spirit world. It turned out alright that time, but it could have just as easily turned out very badly for me.

If you are not in the places where trouble is usually found, you can be fairly assured of your safety. Keep out of range of trouble. Don't tempt fate. Stay clear of people of low character, and you will stay out of range of their attacks.

83

Rely not on the likelihood of the enemy's not coming, but on our own readiness to receive him; not on the chance of his not attacking, but rather on the fact that we have made our position unassailable.

Sun Tzu

You don't really have any control over whether or not some predator decides to mug you or assault you. While it is true that presenting a certain image of confidence and awareness can deter many predators from seeing you as an easy target, you really have no assurance that some low-life will not try to attack you for whatever reason. You can't rely on the enemy not coming. The only thing that you really have total control over is whether or not you will be ready, if and when someone does decide to attack you.

How do you make yourself unassailable and ready to repel an attack from a predator? To start with, make sure you have not neglected your training. Keeping up with your training will continue to keep your self-confidence in your martial arts skills high. This self-confidence will shine through and will not only serve as a deterrence for predators, but will also make them rethink their decision should they actually confront you.

I know that I have said it before, but it is worth repeating at nauseam. Be aware of your surroundings. This is probably the most important factor in making yourself unassailable. If you allow a predator to catch you by surprise, you have put yourself at an automatic disadvantage. Take nothing for granted; make yourself as ready as possible.

84

Tomorrow's battle is won during today's practice.
Samurai Maxim

You never know when you will have to depend on the skills that you have developed during your training. One thing that you can be sure of is that you cannot wait until you need your martial arts skills to start training. It is too late to develop your skills at that point in time. When your enemy attacks, you can't call "time out" to stretch and warm up; you had better be prepared. This is why it is so important to take your training seriously. It is very easy to become complacent in your training, especially when it seems as if you will never actually need to use your martial arts. Don't let this happen.

The warrior has a duty to be in shape and to be ready for whatever may come. He has to be ready to spring into action at a moment's notice. Train today as if you are going to war tomorrow. Remember that whether you decide to practice or not, somewhere out there your enemy is practicing hard, honing his skills, and getting ready for his next victim.

Practice hard. Always keep in mind why you should take your training "deadly serious." You can't wait until the rains come to fix your roof. If you do, you will find you have a lot of leaks and a mess to clean up. The same applies to your training. If you are slacking off during today's practice, you will find that you have a lot of holes in your defense during tomorrow's battle, and maybe a bloody mess to clean up afterwards.

85

Instead of worrying,
a strong man wears a smile.
Japanese Proverb

Worrying serves no purpose whatsoever. It is a total waste of time. The warrior should not allow his mind to be clouded by worrying about what may or may not happen in the future. He must think rationally. If you can do something about the situation at hand, then make a decision about the right course of action and act. If the situation cannot be changed, then let it go and focus on something else. Either way, worrying will not help you resolve your problem.

This is another instance when you have to discipline your mind. Controlling your mind is a skill that is just as important to you as your martial arts skills. Actually, if you can't control your mind, your martial arts skills will falter in a life-and-death situation. You must control your mind. Do what you can do about the situation, know that you have done your best, then let the chips fall where they may. When you have done all that you can do, what else is there?

Realize that you have done your best to live according to your principles. After you have done your best, whatever is going to happen, is going to happen. Worrying will not change that. Calm your mind and know that whatever happens, you will be able to deal with it. When things change, you will see what steps you need to take next, and you will again act to the best of your abilities. For the warrior, life is a series of evaluating the situation, deciding on the right course of action, and then taking the right action.

86

The wise man hides his weapons.
Lao Tzu

Too many people feel the need to announce their skills and their talents everywhere that they go. They just can't seem to control the urge to pat themselves on the back. Not only do they frequently publicize their "amazing" skills, but they usually embellish their skills more and more each time that they recall their "great feats." This is not the way of the warrior.

Lao Tzu taught in the, *Tao Te Ching*, that you shouldn't publicize your skills. Resist the urge to brag on yourself. It is not necessary for everyone to understand how dangerous you really are, or how great your front kick is. In fact, publicizing your skills can only work against you. It gives your enemy a heads up concerning your abilities and your weaknesses. Hide your abilities, your weapons, and your knowledge. Don't let just anyone enter your private world. Be wise.

The great martial arts masters did not teach just anyone. They were very careful about who they shared their knowledge with, especially their advanced skills. Potential students had to prove their loyalty and their good moral character to the master over years and years of dedication and training. Even then, only a very few were considered worthy of learning the master's hidden strategies and techniques. Be very careful about who you trust and who you share your techniques with.

87

No matter what the warrior is doing, he must conduct himself in the manner of a true warrior.
Bushido Shoshinshu

Always maintain your dignity, no matter where you are or what you are doing. It doesn't matter what situation you find yourself in, you should always conduct yourself in the manner of a true warrior. This is excellent advice from this ancient samurai text, better known as *The Code of the Samurai translated by Thomas Cleary*. Whatever you are doing, do it with class. Don't lower your standards. Treat everyone you meet with respect and good manners.

Realize that people do watch how you conduct yourself and that they will judge you according to your actions. Everything that you do is contributing to your reputation, either in a positive way or a negative way. Know how a warrior should conduct himself and then make a point of acting that way until it becomes a natural part of your being.

The warrior doesn't change what he is because of what somebody else is or because of what somebody else does. He remains the same regardless of his environment. His character doesn't change according to the company he happens to find himself surrounded by at the time. No matter where he is or what he is doing, he conducts himself according to his code of ethics, and in the manner of a true warrior.

88

To stand still is to regress.
Gichin Funakoshi

No matter how far you paddle your boat up the river, if you stop paddling you will start to float backwards. You may have a goal to get to a certain place up the river, but once you get to that place, you cannot stay there unless you continue to work to maintain your position. The day you don't feel like paddling to maintain your position, you will find that you have lost some ground and that it will take some work to get back to where you were. You will also find that when you quit paddling, you will go back down the river much faster than you paddled up the river.

There is no standing still in the river. You are either moving toward your goal or you are moving away from your goal. It takes discipline and work to maintain your goal, even after you have obtained it. The warrior is never satisfied achieving his goal and then stopping. You don't get to a certain point in your training and think that you are set for life. Continue to train for perfection and excellence in every area of your life.

When you stop training, you start to regress. The more you regress, the less prepared you are to meet your enemy. Continue to train hard and maintain your level of preparedness. Don't let your skills, which you have worked so hard to achieve, disappear with the current of inactivity.

89

A successful samurai should put his heart in order first thing in the morning and last thing at night.
The Hagakure

The warrior has to "cleanse" his heart just as he has to clean his weapons and keep them in good working order. What I mean by this is that you have to continually make sure that your spirit is free from feelings and emotions that can, and will, move you away from the warrior virtues. Make sure that you do not harbor hate, fear or unforgiveness in your heart. Continually examine yourself to make sure that your motives are pure and just.

As the samurai maxim from *Hagakure: The Book of the Samurai* tells us, one way to do this is to examine your heart first thing in the morning and last thing at night. Take time to pause and look inside. Are you living according to the warrior ideals? Are you upholding your character as a warrior should? Is your heart right? If not, take steps to put your heart in order.

Focus on what your ultimate goal is and determine what needs to be done in order for you to continue on your quest. The journey of the warrior is a never-ending path and requires constant vigilance in order to continue to move forward. Spend time meditating on your actions, your motives, and your thoughts. If you find weeds in your garden, don't just try to keep them under control; remove them completely from the roots.

90

When you see a correct course, act.
Sun Tzu

Too many people can see the right action, but do not have the courage to act. They justify their inaction in a multitude of ways, but it all boils down to a lack of courage. It takes courage to act when nobody is on your side or when taking the right action could cost you in some way. The warrior is always on the side of justice. He focuses on what he should do and not on other people's opinions. Have the courage to do the right thing.

This sounds like common sense and in a way it is, but at the same time this is not as easy as it sounds. For example, if you are walking through the park and you see some thugs are vandalizing someone's car, you know the right thing to do is to question them and not just walk on by, but that takes a lot of courage. It takes a special kind of person to approach and question two thugs who may or may not be dangerous. After all, it is not your car, so what makes it any of your business?

The simple answer is that you are a warrior, and therefore you have a duty to your fellow man to watch his back. You see that what is happening here is wrong. What would you want someone to do if they were walking by and it was your car that these two guys were vandalizing? Would you want someone to just go on with his walk and pretend he didn't even see what was happening or would you want him to say something and get involved? As a warrior, you have a greater responsibility to act than the average man. Take action when action needs to be taken.

91

There is a best way to perform any task.
Bruce Lee

There may be many ways to skin a cat, as the saying goes, but there is only one "best" way. No matter what the task is, there is only one best way to perform that task. At first this may not seem true. You may think that one way is as good as another to get the job done, but this is not quite right. Bruce Lee wrote in his famous book, *The Tao of Jeet Kune Do*, that there is always a single best way to perform any task.

Martial arts practiced correctly, focuses on the most efficient way of taking care of the business at hand, whether it is defending yourself against an attacker or perfecting your front kick. That is why the warrior practices the same kicks and punches over and over until they become second nature. Once these techniques become second nature, they have become efficient and honed to perfection, if they have been practiced correctly. Don't just get the job done. Shoot for perfection. No wasted energy.

It is vital that you practice your skills as they should be performed. Practice does not make perfect; perfect practice makes perfect. Sloppy practice will lead to sloppy techniques, and sloppy techniques can come back to haunt you when you need to use your skills in battle. There is a best way to perform every technique, and this is the way you should practice your art.

92

The warrior is always in training, and to some extent, at some level of consciousness, training is always on his mind.
Forrest E. Morgan

At first glance this statement seems ridiculous. How could anyone always be in training? But when given closer thought, this makes perfect sense, knowing the character of the warrior. He may not be always training physically, but at *some level of consciousness* he is training. If he is driving down the road, he may be visualizing self-defense techniques in his mind or visualizing a dangerous encounter and how he would handle the situation. This is a form of training. Mental training is as important as physical training for the warrior.

There are many examples of warrior training that do not involve actual physical training. While in the movie theater, the warrior may be practicing awareness of his surroundings, while at the same time he is critiquing what the hero could have done differently in order to have ended the conflict better, again a form of mental training.

When you look at training in this light, the admonition by Musashi in, *The Book of Five Rings,* to train more than you sleep becomes a possibility even in today's world. To the warrior, the training possibilities are endless, no matter what he is actually doing. Next time you are doing something other than working on your skills, think about how you could be integrating training into what you are doing. When you look at training in this light, it becomes a very real possibility, even in today's world.

93

Outside noisy, inside empty.
Chinese Proverb

Just as a jug that is empty makes more noise than a jug that is full, people who talk too much usually have less wisdom than the people who say little. People who continually chatter on and on about nothing, have very little wisdom inside to draw from, thus the saying outside noisy, inside empty. The same can be said concerning people who brag about their martial arts skills.

People who go on and on about how tough they are, or how good a fighter they are, usually are trying to convince themselves that they have the skills which they in fact lack. They want you to think that they are something special. In reality, they know that they are not that tough and that they don't have the skills that they wish they had. Outside they present the image of being this great martial arts expert while inside they have the skills of a novice martial artist.

The master warrior, much the same as the master sage, will not brag about his skills. He does his best to perfect his art and leaves it at that. Obtaining the admiration of lesser men is not on his list of goals. He is not concerned with the appearance of being tough or the appearance of being a master; he is focused only on what is, not what appears to be. "Outside noisy, inside empty" refers to the pretender. "Outside quiet, inside secure" refers to the warrior.

94

Both speech and silence transgress.
Zen Maxim

The warrior knows that he must be careful concerning his speech. He knows that it is better to listen and increase his wisdom, than to continually talk and reveal his secrets and lack of knowledge. Furthermore, he knows full well that it is very easy to break the code, which he lives by, when he doesn't control his speech. It is very easy to transgress against the code of the warrior through speech. But what many warriors don't realize is that it is also very easy to break their code of ethics by remaining silent.

Although the warrior is normally silent, he does have a responsibility to speak up when his honor requires that he do so. It is part of his duty to take the side of those who cannot defend themselves and those who righteously need his help. There are many times when, for the warrior, remaining silent is an act of cowardice. There are times when the warrior needs to speak out against prejudice, stupidity, and ignorance, but this doesn't mean that you must always confront every fool who is spouting rubbish.

You have to be discerning about the situation and determine what each circumstance requires you, as a warrior, to do to fulfill your duty. Never argue or debate with a fool, but at the same time don't shy away from saying what needs to be said, when it needs to be said. Say what you have to say and let that be that. To be able to walk through life and not transgress by either speech or silence requires wisdom and practice, and it is a skill that the warrior needs to perfect.

95

He who conquers others is strong; he who conquers himself is mighty.
Lao Tzu

Many of the topics that I have discussed so far in *Warrior Wisdom: Ageless Wisdom for the Modern Warrior* take a lot of practice, wisdom, and discipline to perfect. Much of the requirements of the warrior lifestyle do not come naturally, but rather have to be developed over time. Skills such as controlling your speech, controlling your anger and emotions, being courageous in every situation, and always standing up for the weak and those who are in need of your help, are easier said than done much of the time. It takes a lot of discipline to develop these traits.

The easy part of being a warrior is learning and honing the martial arts skills. This is a demanding, but fun and exciting part of training for the warrior. Once these skills have been perfected, it is easy to conquer others when the circumstance demands it from you. The true warrior is strong in this arena. What makes the warrior mighty though, is not being able to destroy thugs when he has to, but is conquering himself through self-discipline in the other areas of warrior training.

This is much harder to do than becoming proficient in martial arts skills. The skills that you obtain in the quest to conquer yourself are actually used much more frequently than your martial arts skills. You will find opportunities to hone these skills and conquer yourself every day. See irritations as opportunities to conquer your base nature. Believe me, people will find ways to give you the practice that you need to develop patience, kindness and compassion.

96

The superior man seeks what is right; the inferior one, what is profitable.
Confucius

Today it is very rare to find a person who will think about what is right instead of what is "best" for them personally. As I have discussed, the warrior should be a superior man, a man of excellence. Confucius tells us that the superior man will seek what is right, not what is profitable. This doesn't mean that the warrior never seeks what is profitable for himself and his family. What it does mean is that the warrior will not seek what is profitable while at the same time disregarding what is right.

The warrior thinks first about what is right, what is justified, and then what is profitable. You should always seek to do what is right. Sometimes this may not be the most profitable path for you to take. It is easy to profit if you have low standards. Drug dealers profit every day. In fact they make huge profits because they are only concerned with making money, not doing what is right.

The warrior on the other hand is restrained by his ethics and character. He is not free to seek profit by any means available. He answers to his code of ethics. If he feels that an action is not right, he will not act, no matter how profitable that action may be for him. Put what is right before what is profitable; be a superior man.

97

Nobody is undefeatable or indestructible.
Bohdi Sanders

No one is undefeatable. Everyone is human, and as a human being, everyone has the same vulnerable targets. Even the biggest, strongest, toughest thug that you can imagine running into on the street has his weaknesses. David killed Goliath, not by being in better shape or by being better trained, but by keeping his cool and using his mind. Sure he was proficient with his slingshot, but had he panicked at the sight of this giant warrior, he probably would not have had the accuracy needed to defeat his enemy. We are talking about a young boy, killing a seasoned warrior who was supposed to be undefeatable.

In any physical confrontation there are many variables which can totally alter the outcome of the fight. There are an unlimited number of mistakes that can be made, many of which could end the confrontation if the warrior keeps his cool and is able to see the opening. The trick is to always maintain a calm, rational mind-set. Let your training and your spirit guide you. Don't think too much.

Essentially, allow yourself to enter what is known as mushin. Mushin literally means mind-no-mind. Your mind is calm and sharp, but at the same time you are not actively "thinking" about what you should do or what you should not do; your spirit is in control, not your mind. In mushin, all of the training and techniques that you have worked on day after day will flow automatically. The warrior can't allow himself to be psyched-out by the illusion that his opponent is indestructible. Nobody is undefeatable.

98

Great winds are powerless to disturb the water of a deep well.
Chinese Proverb

The warrior should not get annoyed or upset at every little thing that goes wrong in his life. Small things affect small minds. Don't allow things to dictate to you what your emotional state will be. You may be thinking that this is easier said than done, after all, when something bad happens, it is supposed to make you upset or put you in a bad mood. Well, it doesn't have to upset you or affect your mood.

You have to stay calm in your mind. Don't let the winds that blow outside enter your mind and affect your peace and tranquility. You decide what your emotional state will be. It is up to you. As a warrior, you must remain in control. Don't give the control of your emotions to any other person or circumstance. Look at things rationally and calmly, and decide how to handle each situation. Act, don't react. Remain in control at all times.

What's the difference between acting and reacting? Reacting is responding to something or someone according to the feelings that are aroused in you by whatever has happened. Essentially, it is allowing your emotions to dictate your actions. This can get you in trouble. Instead of reacting, you should take rational action. This means that you rationally determine what the right course of action is and then act. This is the way of the warrior.

99

Each action (of the warrior) is performed from a place of fundamental wisdom...it is completely different from the ordinary behavior of a fool. Even if it looks the same, it is different on the inside.
Takuan Soho

This is a very important statement for anyone who seeks to live the warrior lifestyle to contemplate. Every action of the warrior is performed from a place of fundamental wisdom; even if it looks the same on the outside as everybody else's action, it is different. How is it different? It is different on the inside, the intention is different, the spirit is different. You have to look below the surface. Not everything is as it first appears. In fact, things are seldom completely as they seem from the outside, especially where the warrior is concerned.

The warrior may be having a drink with a friend at the local pub and at first glance, he may look the same as the weak-minded fools that are surrounding him in the bar, but even though he may look as though he is the same on the outside, this is just an illusion. He is as different from the others as night is from day. He is coming from a totally different place, a place of fundamental wisdom.

He is different, even though he seems the same. The differences may be hard to distinguish for the ordinary person, but they are there, cloaked behind his unflinching poker face. Don't be too quick to judge someone. You only see what he allows you to see. You don't see the fundamental wisdom contained in his thoughts nor do you know the purpose and intention behind his actions. Think about this.

100

To know and to act are one and the same.
Samurai Maxim

If you truly know something, you will act on it. If you "know" that eating that cheeseburger and fries will clog your arteries and cause you to have a heart attack, you would not eat the cheeseburger and fries. Who in their right mind would eat something "knowing" that it would kill them? But most people still eat that cheeseburger and fries because they do not *really know* this information. If they knew it, they would not eat it. They may have heard it, they may have read it, or they may have been told it, but they don't really "know" it.

The same is true for the warrior ideals. If you "know" that the warrior ideals are the best way to live your life, you will live by them and you will act on them and develop them. But before you act on them and make them a part of your everyday life, you have to really, truly know this. You have to actually believe this or else you will just practice them for a while and gradually, they will fade from your lifestyle, just as you may eat healthy for a while and gradually fall back into your old eating habits.

Meditate on the importance of the warrior ideals until you realize the importance of them. Then you will make these ideals, which you truly know inside your spirit to be true, an integral part of your life. Nothing will become a permanent part of your life unless you truly believe and feel that it holds some intrinsic value for you. The warrior ideals are one of those rare things that will change your life.

101

For opportunity knocks at your door just once, and in many cases you have to decide and to act quickly.
Francesco Guicciardini

There are times when you have to act quickly to take advantage of an opportunity when it presents itself. I enjoy going to yard sales and finding deals. I guess you could say it is one of my hobbies. One Saturday I stopped at a yard sale that had a beautiful bed made of aspen logs. The owner was asking $75 for the bed, but I was indecisive about buying the bed because I really didn't need it and would only be buying it for resale.

I decided to think about it and come back, so I went home to check some prices and found that the exact same bed sells for about $750. Excited about what I found out, I rushed out to buy the bed and make a killing off of this great opportunity, but when I arrived, the bed had already been sold. This is a good example of a golden opportunity lost because of indecision.

When you find an opportunity has opened itself up to you, you have to take advantage of it quickly. You have to be prepared to make a snap decision and act immediately. Opportunities do not last forever. This is especially true if you are facing a physical encounter on the street. When the opportunity presents itself, you have to act quickly and take advantage of it. Once it is gone you may not get a second chance. Think about this.

102

Do nothing evil, neither in the presence of others, nor privately.
Pythagoras

It is fairly easy for most people to refrain from doing evil in public. The majority of the people today are concerned about their reputations and how other people in their community view them. Behaving well in public has been ingrained in them since they were young, although even this seems to be less common in today's society. Behaving well in public is only half of the equation.

Pythagoras also tells us that you must also be careful to avoid doing evil in private. Evil acts are still evil whether they are performed in public or in private. Since the warrior is concerned with perfecting his character, it doesn't matter whether or not someone is watching his actions. What matters is that his actions are right. His overall focus is on the action itself and the intention behind the action, not on what others think about his actions.

The warrior must continually examine not only his behavior, but also the motives behind his behavior. The warrior's intentions must be pure and virtuous. He cannot allow right actions to be spoiled by less than honorable intentions or dishonorable motives. This is the perfection of character that Master Gichin Funakoshi spoke of in his book, *Karate Do-Kyohan*. Make the perfection of your character one of the goals that you strive for in your warrior walk. Live the same honorable life whether it be in private or in public.

103

Virtue is more clearly shown in the performance of fine actions than in the nonperformance of base ones.
Aristotle

You cannot necessarily judge someone's virtue by whether or not that person refrains from doing bad things. Many people refrain from robbing banks because of their fear of being put in prison, not because they are virtuous. If they were assured that they would not be caught and punished, many people would do the very things that they daily refrain from doing and which they loudly condemn others for doing. Their restraint does not testify to their virtue.

As Aristotle states, if you want to judge a person's virtue, look at what they do, not at what they refrain from doing. A man's virtue is shown more clearly by his actions, and even more so by the intentions behind those actions. The character of every action depends on the circumstances and the intentions behind the action.

Look beneath the surface when trying to judge someone's character. What is the motivation behind the action or the lack of action? As a warrior, you must make sure that you do the right thing, for the right reason. Keep your virtue intact. Live by your own ideals. Hold yourself to the highest standards.

104

If it is not right, do not do it;
if it is not true, do not say it.
Marcus Aurelius

Marcus Aurelius makes warrior ethics as straightforward as possible with this statement. It pretty much says it all. "If it is not right, do not do it; if it is not true, do not say it." That doesn't leave much grey area. The warrior must strive to do what is right, but how does he know what is right and what is not right? Does the warrior look to the law to decide what is right and what is wrong? What about areas that aren't covered in the law?

There are many actions, which are not against the law, that the real warrior would consider dishonorable. So what guides the warrior as far as what is right and what is wrong? He depends on his sense of honor and his code of ethics. Sometimes he may have to actually break the law in order to act within his code of honor. At the same time, there may be many things which our law permits that the warrior's own code does not permit him to do.

The warrior lives by his own code of ethics. It is a higher, more demanding standard than the law of the land. He knows in his heart what is right and what is wrong. He has developed this "knowing" through meditation, discipline, and living the warrior lifestyle. If it is not right, don't do it - enough said.

105

The man of principle never forgets what he is, because of what others are.
Baltasar Gracian

The warrior is a man of principle. He doesn't set his principles aside when they do not seem convenient. Today many people do just that. They use the actions of others to justify their own bad behavior. Statements such as, "Well I wouldn't have done that if he hadn't shoved me, cursed me, etc." are commonly heard to justify wrong behavior. The warrior should not allow the behavior of others to affect his behavior, as far as doing things that are against his principles.

The warrior never forgets who he is or what he is, because of what others are or what others do. If someone is acting like a jerk, that doesn't give you a free pass to set aside your principles. Someone else's actions have nothing to do with you. You are responsible for your actions, not someone else's actions.

Someone else being what they are, whether it is a jerk, a criminal, or whatever, should not cause you to forget who you are, and that is a man of principle. Don't allow the actions of others to cause you to compromise your principles. This is an easy trap to walk into. Think rationally and remember who you are and what you are. The man of principle never forgets what he is.

106

You must carefully consider the merits of any action, and if you then take the good and leave the bad, your mind will naturally become more virtuous.
Takuan Soho

In order for the warrior to ensure that his actions are just, he must think about his actions *before* he actually acts. You shouldn't act mindlessly, just doing whatever pops into your head. You must give thought to your actions. Think about the consequences of your actions before you act. Ponder the motives and intentions behind the action.

If you do these things, your actions will logically become more and more virtuous, and you will find that you are making fewer mistakes. Acts which you wish that you hadn't done will become fewer and fewer. You will find that your character will naturally start to move toward the ultimate goal of perfection. Think before you act.

Your actions ultimately define who you are. As Emerson said, "Your actions are a picture book of your creed." Your honor and your character will determine your actions, and your actions are a window in which others are allowed to judge your character. Others are never actually able to perceive your intentions, but your actions will be scrutinized closely. Leave them no room to question your character.

107

**A wise man, in great or small matters,
must act with due consideration.
Whether attacking a hare or an elephant,
the lion has no time for indecision.**
Sakya Pandit

The warrior has no time for indecision. He must know the right course to take, and then act accordingly, without delay. Indecision can bring about defeat. It can cloud the mind and confuse the thought process. Have confidence in your judgment and act decisively. Deliberate often, but decide once. Once your decision is made, follow through to the end. Going back and forth, and changing your mind time and again, accomplishes little more than to add to your uncertainty concerning what you should do.

It doesn't matter what you are debating or what the issue at hand happens to be, habitual indecision only makes things worse. This doesn't mean that you should rush to make a decision. On the contrary, timing is essential. The right decision at one moment may be the wrong decision just a few minutes later.

Even small matters require your full consideration. A small slip while in the middle of a violent confrontation could cost you dearly. When you see it is time to strike, you must strike immediately. Things change constantly in battle and delaying your attack may render your attack useless. Once the opportunity is gone, it is gone forever. Indecision can defeat you both in battle and in life.

108

Reflect on this:
efforts and enemies, if left unfinished, can
both ravage you like an unextinguished fire.
Tiruvalluvar

When you start something, finish it. Don't leave anything undone. The warrior must strive for excellence in all that he does. He must give his best all of the time, every time. Tiruvalluvar is trying to stress the importance of this in the above quote. Warriors realize the importance of making sure that your enemy is completely defeated before you stop your attack, but by combining "effort" and "enemies" in the same category, Tiruvalluvar is demanding that we look beyond our enemy to the bigger picture.

You must grapple with the fact that your lack of effort and attention can derail your goals on the path of the warrior, just as an unfinished enemy can overturn your victory during a physical confrontation. The warrior lifestyle requires both attention to details and constant effort in order to make it part of your being. Without the proper effort towards this lofty goal, it will remain unobtainable.

Finish what you start. Don't leave things half-way done. Anything worth doing is worth doing well. Whether you are getting a hard workout or going head to head with a dangerous adversary, stay focused to the end. Niccolo Machiavelli taught in this book *The Prince,* that you should never leave an enemy standing. When you have a fire to put out, make sure you leave no danger of it re-igniting. Give some thought to this.

109

When you see a rattlesnake poised to strike, you do not wait until he has struck before you crush him.
Franklin Delano Roosevelt

Gichin Funakoshi stated that there is no first attack in karate, but what exactly does this mean? Does this mean that you cannot throw a kick or a punch until your enemy has tried to kick or hit you first? No, this is a misconception. An attack does not necessarily have to be physical. Many times, waiting until the first kick or punch has been thrown is a mistake. It is rare that an enemy just walks up and throws a punch without any warning. There is usually a verbal or a visual attack that precedes an actual physical attack. The warrior should be able to sense imminent danger.

When you have determined that you or someone else is in danger, the first attack has already occurred. Once you have reached that point, you decide when it is time to strike. Don't wait for the enemy to set the pace or make his move. You be in control. Read the situation and take the appropriate action at the appropriate time. When you know that danger is imminent, and that an engagement is unavoidable, then it is time for you to act. Be decisive and crush your enemy before he can harm you. Be aware and learn to sense danger. Listen to your inner spirit and have the confidence to act on what it tells you.

110

Think of the going out before you enter.
Arabian Proverb

Always think ahead. Think about all the possible scenarios before you get yourself into something. Try to always leave yourself a safety valve or a backdoor. A warrior should inevitably have a "plan B" up his sleeve just in case things go wrong. This is not to say that he plans for failure, but he is prepared for whatever may happen and is able to respond to the changing environment.

Don't get caught off guard because you rashly entered into a situation without thinking about the possible consequences and how you will deal with those consequences should they arise. Think ahead. Do not get yourself into circumstances where you have no way out. This is a very dangerous position for a warrior to be caught in at any time. The warrior should never be at the mercy of others as far as his choices go.

You avoid placing yourself in these kinds of situations by thinking ahead. Look beyond the obvious and see the hidden facets of everything. Don't commit to something before you have investigated it thoroughly. Know the "ins" and "outs" before you enter into any state of affairs. Be careful who you accept favors from; you don't want to be indebted to someone of low character. Think of the possible ending point before you begin anything.

111

One who is good at being a warrior does not appear formidable.
Lao Tzu

Lao Tzu points out in the *Tao Te Ching*, that it is not necessary to look fierce and formidable in order to be a good warrior. In fact, looking like the ultimate warrior can have some definite drawbacks. There are many people out there who are intimidated by someone who looks like a gladiator and others who feel compelled to challenge the warrior to prove their "manhood." The warrior who does not appear formidable on the surface automatically has several advantages.

Think of the *Karate Kid* movies. Mr. Miyagi was certainly a warrior, but he did not seem formidable. No one would be tempted to challenge this "old man" to prove their prowess in the fighting arts. He definitely would not be intimidating to others, as far as his looks were concerned. And yet he was a formidable warrior. His deceptive looks gave him an advantage over his would be enemies because no one expected him to be a warrior. They were always caught off guard by his skills and knowledge.

Develop the skills, knowledge and discipline of a warrior, and don't worry about your appearance or image. Be concerned with authenticity, not appearances. You do not have to prove anything to anybody, except yourself. Once you know on the inside who you really are and what you can do, it doesn't matter what anyone else thinks. Their opinions will not affect you anymore. Be satisfied with the knowledge of who you are and don't feel the need to show others.

112

You may always be victorious if you will never enter into any contest where the issue does not wholly depend upon yourself.
Epictetus

Epictetus seems to be stating the obvious in this quote, but does this quote really apply to the warrior? Can the warrior never enter into any contest where the issue does not wholly depend upon him? Well, the answer is yes and no. In situations such as war, the answer is no, but for the purposes of one's personal life, the answer is yes, you can determine exactly which "contest" you will enter, and when and how you will enter that contest.

Don't just rush into a situation. Think about all the possible consequences before you jump into a conflict. Of course there are times when duty demands that the warrior act on the spur of the moment, but by using your mind, you can still make the outcome depend wholly on yourself.

Your mind is your best weapon. There will not be many times when you will be required to act on the spur of the moment. All other times, you make the decision concerning whether to take action or not. Use your mind and determine the best course of action to take. Don't enter into a confrontation if you know there is a better way to end the conflict or a more advantageous time to make your stand. Be smart, not foolhardy.

113

Even in the sheath the knife must be sharp.
Finnish Proverb

Your martial arts training must be kept sharp. It is one of the duties of the warrior to keep his skills ready at all times. Don't neglect your training. It is easy to fall into the mental illusion that you may never really need to use your martial arts skills in "real life," but as a warrior, you cannot think this way.

As the above proverb states, "Even in the sheath the knife must be kept sharp." The same goes for your martial arts skills; even if you are not using them, and they are "just in the sheath," they still must be sharp. You don't wait until you need your knife to clean it up and sharpen it. After you use it, you clean it, sharpen it and store it in good shape for the next time you need to use it.

In the same way, you don't wait until you need your martial arts skills to make sure they are developed, sharp and ready to be used. You keep them sharp and ready to be used when you need them. Procrastination can be a deadly habit. The warrior's weapons are kept sheathed the majority of the time, but they still have to be kept sharp. You don't want to find that you need to use your "knife" and when you take it out of the sheath, it is dull, rusted, and couldn't cut hot butter. Think about this.

114

Do nothing to make you lose respect for yourself, or to cheapen yourself in your own eyes; let your own integrity be the standard of rectitude, and let your own dictates be stricter than the precepts of any law.
Baltasar Gracian

You should never do anything that will cause you to lose your self-respect. You must maintain your self-respect at all times. Don't lower your standards because of fear or because everyone is pressuring you to do something. It takes courage to stand for what you believe when it seems that everyone else is taking the opposite stance. You must find the courage to stand firm. Backing down when you know you are right chips away at your self-respect.

Set your own standards of right and wrong. The warrior does what is right no matter what anyone else does. He lives by the code which he sets down for himself and this code is stricter than any law of the land. He lives by his code of integrity and refuses to break it to please the crowd. He knows what he stands for and refuses to bend where his principles are concerned. This attitude will always keep your self-respect intact.

It is always a mistake to compromise on your standards for any reason, but it is extremely foolish to compromise your standards to please someone else. Your favor with them will only be temporary and your disappointment with yourself will last much longer. If your friends do not accept you for who you are without trying to get you to make concessions where your standards are concerned, then they are not truly your friends. Put your integrity first.

115

Keep your distance from unvirtuous people.
Takuan Soho

Associating with less than virtuous, low class people will always interfere with your goals as a warrior. It may not be obvious at first, but take my word for it; they will never help you on your path, and many times can severely sidetrack your journey. One of my students, who I have known for many years and I personally know to be a good guy, found the truth behind the principle the hard way.

This student started to pal around with the wrong kind of people, people who partied too much and were involved in drugs. He later found out that his so-called "friends" were also dealing drugs, but he thought that it was alright as long as he wasn't the one dealing illegal drugs. His attitude towards the whole drug culture began to change as he spent more and more time with these people, after all, these were his "friends."

One night his "friends" threw a backpack into the trunk of his car as they hitched a ride home from a party. This student found himself pulled over by the police for speeding and guess what the police found in his trunk - several pounds of drugs and drug paraphernalia. Did his "friends" come to his rescue or did they let him take the fall for the drugs found in the trunk of his car? What do you think?

I will give you a hint: this student no longer has a driver's license or a car, but he does have a criminal record now. His "friends" went on with their life without giving the incident a second thought, other than to use it as an occasional amusing story. Be careful about who you associate with and who you call your friend.

116

Beware a dagger hidden in a smile.
Shi Nai'an

You have to develop the instinct of knowing who to trust and who not to trust. There are a lot of bad people out there and many of them know how to con people into trusting them. They have great personalities and can be fun to be around, but hidden beneath their smile is a different agenda. Don't look at the outside appearances, but look deeper beneath the surface. See things as they really are, not as they appear to be.

Know that people who have malicious intentions are smart enough to hide their intentions with their friendly personalities and their winning smiles. Don't be too quick to trust people. Always evaluate the situation from every angle. Remember that not everyone that you meet lives by the same code of standards that you live by. In fact, the vast majority of people out there do not live by the strict standards of right and wrong that the warrior sets for himself.

Most people make their decisions strictly on what is best for them. If they want something, they have learned how to use their wit and personality to manipulate people and get what they want. They have become so proficient at this that they no longer have to make an effort to manipulate people; it comes naturally for them, just as any skill practiced over a long period of time will become a part of you. Always think about what is going on in the other person's mind and beware of the dagger hidden in his smile. Think about this.

117

Lay down for yourself, at the outset, a certain stamp and type of character for yourself, which you are to maintain whether you are by yourself or are meeting with people.
Epictetus

You may be thinking that it must be exhausting having to make all these decisions every day concerning what is right and what is wrong, as you walk the path of the warrior. But that is really not the way it is. The warrior does not have to mentally debate every issue that comes along to decide which action is right or wrong. The issue of how the warrior will live has already been decided. He has already set the standards that he will live by, and he knows what he stands for and what he will not stand for. These decisions have already been made.

What the warrior must do on a daily basis is *actually live* by the standards that he has set for himself. He knows what is right and what is wrong, and he knows that it is his duty to maintain his character and to have the courage to do what is right. His code is not for show. He doesn't use it to impress people. It is his way of life. It is who he is.

The warrior knows all of this. All that is left for him to do is to put all these things into action. Whether he is alone or with others, he must live up to his standards. He has determined the type of character that he wants for himself, and he knows in order to develop and maintain that character, he must make it a vital part of who he is, whether alone or with other people. Make a firm decision concerning how you will live your life, and stick to it.

118

Hear all sides and you will be enlightened.
Hear one side, and you will be in the dark.
Wei Zheng

Everyone perceives things through their own lens. There are very few people who can give you an unbiased opinion on any subject. If you have five people who witness a fight, you will get five different accounts of what happened, maybe not on the main points, but they will differ concerning the details. For this reason, it is always wise to hear all sides of the story before you form any opinions.

True life court shows on television demonstrate this fact. They will go through the evidence and present the prosecution's side of the case, and you think to yourself, "this guy is guilty as sin," but when the defense presents their case, many times you start to see things in a different light. Don't be too quick to form a decision. Once you have heard all sides of the issue, then you can form your opinion concerning the matter at hand.

Strive to see things as they really are, not as they appear. Look for the truth. Too many people make decisions without having all of the pertinent information needed to come to a wise conclusion. Without all the information, you're just guessing. Don't be too quick to totally trust the information that you receive from someone else. Trust but verify. Don't be duped, hear all sides before you make important decisions. Make sure that what you think is truly what you think, and not simply someone else's thoughts which have been seeded in your mind.

119

It isn't quite the same thing to comment on the bull ring and to be in the bull ring.
Spanish Proverb

Training is important to the warrior. In fact, it is a vital part of being a warrior. A warrior should train in various self-defense techniques and should be physically fit. He should learn how to respond to various attacks. At the same time he should realize that there is a huge difference between training in a dojo with a safe partner and with specific, scripted techniques, and fighting for your life in a real-life street fight with no rules.

Not every warrior has the experience of being in a real fight, much less a life-or-death situation. It is not the same thing at all. In order to prepare for the real thing, training should be as realistic as possible. I'm not saying that our training should be full contact, all out, anything goes, but it should prepare us mentally, physically, and emotionally for what we may face in the street. If the warrior's training doesn't leave him prepared, it is leaving him with a false sense of security.

Thinking you are prepared to defend yourself, when your skills are not up to par, is a dangerous position to be in. Not only do you need to have confidence in your martial arts skills when you are confronted on the street, but that confidence has to be rooted in ability. There are many people who are confident in their abilities, but their confidence is misplaced. Make sure your confidence is rooted in reality

120

Right is right, even if nobody does it.
Wrong is wrong, even if everybody is wrong about it.
G. K. Chesterson

There is an inscription on the walls of the Catacombs that reads, "The just man is himself his own law." This essentially means that the man of character sets his own rules about right and wrong. If he knows something is right, he will act on it, even if nobody else agrees with his assessment of the situation. Likewise, if he knows something is wrong, he refrains from doing it and stands against it, even if all others claim that he is mistaken in his point of view.

It takes a lot of courage to go against the views of the majority, but that is exactly what the warrior has to do in order to live up to the standards which he sets for himself. The majority is often wrong. Baltasar Gracian said that, "The stupid make up the majority," and "Fools all who seem it, and the half of those who do not." You must decide for yourself what is right and what is wrong. Don't gage the validity of anything by the majority's opinions on the subject.

A warrior must be clear about his own beliefs. He must know what he believes and why he believes it, in order to have the conviction that it takes to stand alone for justice. How can you be motivated enough to stand alone against injustice if you aren't 100% sure about what is right and what is wrong? You must be able to recognize injustice when you see it in order to stand for justice. Always do what is right, even if nobody else does.

121

Because a human being is so malleable, whatever one cultivates is what one becomes.
Lao Tzu

Lao Tzu tells us in the *Tao Te Ching*, that whatever you cultivate, whatever you practice, you become. You have to be careful of your thoughts and your actions. Your thoughts become your actions, your actions become your habits, and your habits become your character. Be aware of what kind of character traits you are cultivating and make sure that they are the character traits of a warrior. If you have cultivated something in your garden that you don't want growing there, take steps to remove it from the roots. Keep your garden weed free. Don't keep the weeds under control, remove them.

Science tells us that it takes anywhere from 30 to 45 days for something to become a habit. That is, if you want to make something a part of your life, practice it for 30 to 45 days, without skipping a day. This fixes that behavior in your mind and essentially causes it to become a habit. It doesn't matter what the behavior is. Your mind and body do not discriminate. They will accept whatever you decide to cultivate.

For this reason it is important that you carefully consider your actions, especially the actions which are part of your daily routine. Bad habits are easy to develop; quality habits take more discipline, at least in the beginning. After something becomes a habit, it takes very little effort to continue to make it part of your life. It becomes natural and essentially automatic. This is the point that you want to reach in your character training, as well as the other vital parts of the warrior lifestyle.

122

In the beginner's mind there are many possiblities, but in the expert's mind there are few.
Shunryu Suzuki

This is an interesting quote and can be applied to the warrior's mind. In the mind of the ordinary person the possibilities concerning how to conduct himself are endless, but to the warrior the possibilities concerning how to conduct himself are few. He is bound by honor and integrity. The same goes for the world's view concerning right and wrong. The world views right and wrong as an endless parade of possibilities depending on what is best for specific issues. The warrior views right and wrong in more concrete terms.

To the beginner, there are many possibilities, but the expert knows that there are only few possibilities because he has wisdom concerning what should be done and what should not be done. He knows what will work and what won't work. It is the same with the warrior. He knows that "give peace a chance" doesn't work when confronted with a violent situation.

Of course there are always many possibilities, but what Shunryu Suzuki is referring to is viable possibilities. The warrior knows that there may be many options in a violent situation, but there are only a few that will keep him and his loved ones safe. This is the difference between an experienced warrior and a novice. The expert warrior knows what must be done in any given situation, or is able to discern what must be done quickly, whereas the beginner is unsure concerning the "many possibilities." This is where constant training comes into play. Think about this.

123

Deal solely with men of honor.
Baltasar Gracian

The advice given by Baltasar Gracian in his classic book, *The Art of Worldly Wisdom*, is to deal solely with men of honor, which may be even better if it stated that you should only trust men of honor. During your journey through this life, you will have to deal with many different people and the majority of them will not be honorable. You have to learn how to read people and know whether or not they are men of honor.

Though you have to deal with all sorts of people, you should only allow men of honor to actually become your close friends. Have many acquaintances, but few real friends. Know the difference between friends and acquaintances. Most people have a hard time realizing the difference between the two and are surprised to find, when their back is against the wall, that they really don't have the friends that they thought they had. Make your true friends men of honor. Men of honor are men you can count on when the chips are down.

It is a very deceptive mistake to think that your acquaintances are true friends. They may be fun to hang out with and interesting to talk to during dinner, but this doesn't mean that they are your true friends. Just because the waiter at your favorite restaurant knows your name, pats you on the back and smiles whenever he sees you, don't make the mistake of thinking that he is your friend.

He has an agenda and that is to have you leave a big tip. The majority of the people you know have agendas. They may not be evil or malicious agendas, but they have personal agendas nonetheless.

124

Every moment of life is the last.
Basho

This is a profound quote by Basho, the 17th century Japanese poet. All you have is the present moment and when that moment is gone, there is no getting it back, it is gone forever. Things are constantly changing, you will never relive this moment in time. Keep in mind that life is very short and fleeting. In a flash you will find yourself in an older body, not able to do what you used to be able to do. Don't waste the present moment. Train as if you were going to fight for your life tomorrow. Enjoy life now. Live your life; don't just go through the motions.

The samurai warriors spent time contemplating their own death. This process allowed them to continuously remember that life is precious and unpredictable. They never knew when they would be required to lay down their life. By contemplating death, the samurai warrior realized the importance of living every moment to the fullest. The samurai's daimyo, his feudal lord, could command the samurai to commit suicide at anytime. He knew that every moment of life had to be lived as if it were his last.

Realize that if you waste this moment in time, it is gone. You can't decide that you don't feel like using this moment right now and put it on the shelf for later. You either use it or you lose it. Use the time which you have been blessed with, and make the most out of every day. This is the way of the warrior. This is Bushido.

125

Only one who continually reexamines himself and corrects his faults will grow.
The Hagakure

Anyone seeking to perfect his character has to continually examine himself in order to correct the things in his life that need to be corrected. All men have faults. Every man has his own personal shortcomings, yes, even the best trained warriors and men of honor have faults that they need to continually keep in check and correct. This is just part of being human. One of the differences between the warrior and other men is that he continually tries to correct his faults, instead of just ignoring them. He is not satisfied allowing them to control his life or parts of his life.

He continually examines himself and molds his life in the way that he knows he should live. Every morning recall the code that you strive to live by, and every night reflect on whether or not you have been successful in living up to your code of honor. Look for ways in which you have fallen short in your quest and determine what you should have done differently, and know that you will handle that situation differently the next time. Strive to improve your life and your character every day.

Little by little your character will be perfected, just as drop by drop the water wears away the stone. Be patient with yourself and continue with your quest. Successes, whether in the warrior lifestyle or any other endeavor, consist of not giving up. Don't quit, just continue to press on with each new day. Every day is a new chance to start with a clean slate.

126

Life is short and no one knows what the next moment will bring.
Dogen

Today is the day to make those new changes in your life that you have been thinking of making. The act of procrastination is essentially an act of robbing yourself. You don't know what the next moment will bring or if there will even be a next moment for you. This is a fact that all of the sages throughout the ages have taught. Everyone knows that they must die sometime, and no one can be sure that they will not die today.

This is not a dress rehearsal. You are not practicing and learning what to do better next time or what you should not do next time around. This is it. You must seize the day and make the most of every minute. Living life tomorrow is living life one day too late. Don't take my word for it, go out and talk to an elderly man and see what he has to say on the subject.

Sai Baba, the Indian holy man, put it this way. "When you are intent upon a journey, after you purchase your ticket and board the train – whether you sit quietly, lie down, read or meditate, the train will take you to the destination. So, too, at birth each living thing has received a ticket to the event of death and is now on the journey." It doesn't matter what you do, as far as time is concerned, the sands still flow. You don't really have a choice about how much time you have, but you do have a choice about how you use that time. Life is short even if it is long. Don't waste it.

127

Let him who desires peace prepare for war.
Vegetius

I have already discussed how important it is to be prepared to defend yourself in order to avoid being identified as a target by a dangerous predator. Predators are experts at picking out an easy target. The sentiment that strength deters your enemy's will to attack has been taught throughout the ages, which is a pretty good indicator that it is a valid strategy.

It may give you that warm, fuzzy feeling to sit around the campfire and sing Kumbaya and discuss how we should all show love and "turn the other cheek," but that is not going to deter any hardcore predator from his twisted plans. Being sweet and nice may work if you are dealing with someone with a conscience, but when you are dealing with people who lack any sense of morality, all they understand is strength and power. All people are not the same, no matter how much people want to think that they are.

The news is full of examples of predators who take advantage of frail elderly women and innocent, defenseless children. Do you honestly think that these people will have a change of heart because you show them love or "turn the other cheek?" You must learn how your enemy thinks. In his classic book on military strategy, *The Art of War*, Sun Tzu teaches us that if you know your enemy and know yourself; in a hundred battles you will never be in peril. Your enemy only understands strength. Show your strength and he will seek easier prey.

128

A small hole can sink a big ship.
Russian Proverb

It is very easy to neglect the weak areas of your training. It is much more fun to train on a kick in which you have mastered and enjoy, than to work on a kick which you don't like and which you are not very proficient. But the kick that you are not very good with is the one that needs the work. Strive, to the best of your ability, to make sure that you have no holes in your defense. Remember, a small hole can sink a big ship.

It will not take very long for an experienced fighter to spot your weakness. It only takes a couple of feints for someone to evaluate how you will react to certain attacks. If he throws a couple of kicks or a couple of punches and you have a weak spot in your defense, it will stand out like a flashing neon sign which says strike here. It doesn't have to be a major weakness in order to cause you major problems.

For example, if you can't kick with your right leg or you constantly hold your right arm too low, that could be enough of a hole to allow your enemy to defeat you. Some weaknesses in your techniques you can spot and correct yourself. Others can only be pointed out to you by your training partner. What you don't want is for that small hole in your defense to be pointed out to you by your enemy in a life-or-death clash. Don't ignore your weak spots. They don't go away just because you refuse to acknowledge them.

129

The warrior acts first according to his heart and his sense of righteousness.
Kensho Furuya

Can you imagine a warrior seeing his friend being pounded by three thugs in an alley, and before he intervenes, he stops and debates whether or not he really wants to hassle with the possibility of someone pressing charges if he hurts them? Of course not! He knows what is right and he acts. He takes the appropriate action immediately and deals with the consequences knowing that he has done the right thing. He actually has no choice; it is his duty as a warrior.

Anytime people start to discuss what is right and what is wrong, someone inevitably brings up the question of who determines what is right. For the warrior, the answer is he determines what is right by listening to his heart. His highly developed sense of ethics guides him and is his true source of righteousness. He learns to listen and trust in the guidance that his heart provides.

Whether you call it your intuition, your inner voice, or something else, the important thing is that you learn to trust in your own sense of righteousness. The warrior must be able to discriminate between right and wrong. This is developed over time and through both long hours of study and meditation. Listen to the teachings of the elders. Their words of wisdom are still valid today, even if the majority of people don't consider them relevant. Once you have a strong sense of right and wrong, you will be ready to act immediately, with full confidence that your actions are right.

130

It is only the tranquil mind that can allow for fair and clear judgments free of error.
Gichin Funakoshi

For thousands of years, sages have taught us to look inside for the answers that we seek. We find this wisdom repeated throughout different cultures from the Native Americans to the earliest wisdom texts. Meditation or retreating to a space of solitary silence, has been used throughout the ages as a way to solve difficult problems and to deal with confusing situations. Silence quiets the mind and allows for clear thinking.

The opposite is also true. Chaos creates a mind full of stress, which causes indecision and confusion. In his classic book *Karate-Do Kyohan*, Gichin Funakoshi tells us that you can only think clearly and rationally if your mind is tranquil. Therefore it is vital that you learn to keep your mind calm, no matter what is happening around you. You must be able to think clearly in order to make rational decisions and sound judgments.

When panic sets in, your mind doesn't function rationally. This is when mistakes are made. Practice keeping yourself calm despite what is happening. The man, who can remain calm while others are panicked, has a distinct advantage over those who have allowed panic to control their mind. This is why warriors throughout history have used fear as an effective form of warfare. Once their enemies allowed fear to enter their minds, their thinking became flawed and they were vulnerable. Knowing this, the warrior must take heed to keep his mind calm and tranquil, and not let the same ploy be played on him.

131

Invincibility depends on one's self; the enemy's vulnerability on him.
Sun Tzu

Your invincibility, your self-defense, depends on you. Ultimately you decide how invincible you will make yourself. The same goes for your enemy. He is vulnerable when he makes a mistake and when he lets his guard down, and so are you. You may be thinking right now that this is ridiculous, there are many really bad people out there who could defeat me on the street. They are bigger and stronger, etc. I have no choice about whether I am vulnerable to them; it's just the way it is. Wrong!

You have a choice of where you go, who you associate with, how you use your mind, how you train, etc. You choose how protected you will be. You decide. Self-defense involves more than knowing how to fight and how to use your martial arts effectively. It involves being smart and using your mind as well. Everything matters in matters of self-defense.

If someone is obviously too skilled for you to handle, then you have to use your wit and your speed to ensure your invincibility. This is just one example of making yourself invincible. The point here is that the choices that you make determine how invincible or how vulnerable you are. It totally depends on you. If you find yourself engaged in a conflict where you are very vulnerable, it is because you made the wrong decisions leading up to that conflict. Give some thought to this.

132

A man must decide what to do, he must go all the way, but he must take responsibility for what he does. No matter what he does, he must know first why he is doing it, and then he must proceed with his actions without having doubts or remorse about them.

Don Juan

This quote by Don Juan fits the warrior perfectly. The warrior must decide what is right and once he has made that decision, he must act, not timidly, but whole-heartedly. He must go all out, holding nothing back. He can go all out and proceed with his whole mind, body and spirit because he knows exactly why he is doing what he is doing. There is no doubt in his mind about why he has to act, and no debate concerning whether or not his action is just. He knows in his heart what action must be taken.

Moreover, he has no remorse or doubts about his actions afterwards. He has done the best that he could do, holding nothing back. He knows in his heart that his actions were righteous, so he is willing to take the responsibility for those actions. The warrior lives by a code of honor that allows him to know without a doubt, what action duty requires him to take.

This insight can only come through the perfection of his character, honor, and integrity, and has to be developed continually. It takes courage and self-confidence to step out and do what must be done. It also takes these traits to be able to proceed without having doubts or remorse about one's actions. Taking responsibility for your actions is a part of being honorable. When you know that your actions were just, taking responsibility for those actions is easy.

133

Be careful of your thoughts;
they are the beginning of your acts.
Lao Tzu

Many people think that their thoughts really don't matter as long as they don't act on the negative or inappropriate thoughts, but thoughts have energy. In the *Tao Te Ching,* Lao Tzu tells us that you need to be careful of your thoughts. Your thoughts are the beginning of your actions. Keeping your mind clear and calm is part of a warrior's training. You should strive to keep your thoughts on a level plain because your thoughts can and do affect your emotions. As I have said before, you cannot afford to allow your emotions to control your actions.

You have to be rational. Keep your thoughts rational. Keep your purpose in mind and focus on what will achieve your goals. Will getting angry help you achieve your goal? Will being upset and dwelling on what has just happened change anything? No, that is living in the past. You can only deal with your problems and decide on the right action to take by being rational and focusing your thoughts on rational solutions.

This is one reason why the warrior should study and meditate on the wisdom of the past. By keeping your thoughts on things which focus on honor and integrity, you allow these qualities to filter down to your actions. When inappropriate thoughts pop into your mind, stop them in their tracks. Don't give them a chance to develop roots and turn into actions. Controlling your thoughts is one of the hardest challenges you will have in your training, but it is vitally important.

134

Beware that you do not lose the substance by grasping at the shadow.
Aesop

As a warrior, you have to see things as they really are, not just as they appear to be. The majority of people are moved by hollow appearances of things. Just look at how many people actually believe the empty campaign rhetoric spewed out by politicians each year. Don't be like the sheep that just go along, believing whatever is presented to them as the truth. Look beyond the shadow and see the substance that is casting the shadow.

It is easy to lose the substance by grasping at the shadow. Fish never see the hook, only the bait. You have to remain aware. Don't be conned. Don't allow your attention to be side tracked to the shadow, while the substance goes unnoticed. This is what seems to happen to the majority of the people; they focus on the shadow instead of the physical reality.

The substance of your martial arts is self-defense and character training. The shadows are tournaments, perfecting your forms, points, decorum, etc. I'm not saying that all of these things do not have a place in the martial arts, but the warrior must never mistake these things for the actual purpose of his training. Don't be caught striving to appear to be a warrior, be a warrior. Cultivate the root and the leaves and branches will take care of themselves.

135

To return to the root is to find the meaning, but to pursue appearances is to miss the source.
Seng Ts'an

Are you honorable or do you just appear to be honorable? Many things in this world are not black and white. There are a lot of grey areas, but being honorable is not one of them. Don't pursue the appearance of being honorable, pursue the real thing. Be honorable and don't worry about how you appear to others. If the truth be told, the majority of people do not know what true honor is to start with, so why would you strive to appear honorable to someone who has no real understanding of the meaning of honor?

It is not your duty to appear honorable to the rest of the world. It is your duty to be honorable period. To live with honor, you first have to be clear concerning what honor really is. You have to return to the root and find the true meaning of honor. What does true honor really entail?

One of the definitions of honor is, "a code of integrity, strong moral character or strength, and adherence to ethical principles." This is what honor means to the warrior. The warrior lives by his own personal code of honor. He determines his honor. He lives his code and does what honor requires without much concern for whether the right action *appears* right to those who do not know. Return to the root of honor and discover the true meaning.

136

So live your life that the fear of death can never enter your heart.
Tecumseh

How do you live your life so the fear of death can never enter your heart? The answer is to live your life to the fullest, leaving nothing undone. You must live your life full throttle. Live with gusto. Be adventurous and experience what life has to offer. Really experience life and at the same time, do it all with a sense of honor and character.

If you aren't living according to your code of honor, then you will sense that you are not living life as you should. This is when the fear of death starts to enter your heart. When you know that you aren't living according to the standards that you have set for yourself, you know that you aren't prepared to meet death.

The warrior who knows that he has lived up to his code of honor and has done the very best that he could do, has few regrets and little fear of death. He knows that his affairs are in order; spiritually, mentally, and physically. He has lived life as it should be lived. Knowing that he has done his best in every endeavor, the warrior has no regrets and therefore is satisfied with his life. This doesn't mean that he welcomes death, but only that he is as prepared for death as possible.

137

Trust your instinct to the end,
though you can render no reason.
Ralph Waldo Emerson

The warrior has to trust his instinct, even if it goes against what everyone else thinks is right. Warriors must be able to count on their own sense of right and wrong, and be able to choose the right course of action. This only comes with time. You have to develop confidence in your own intuition. Your intuition will not lead you in the wrong direction, but you do have to learn how to listen to it, and how to trust in it.

A few years back my wife and I were both teaching school in a small school district in Missouri. We were not happy there and wanted to get back to the Rocky Mountains, but couldn't find teaching positions for the both of us in the same area. The choice was for us to stay where we were or just pick up, pack a truck, and move back to Colorado without any jobs. Now this would seem like an obvious choice to most people - keep your job. But we decided to listen to our instinct instead.

Our instinct told us it was time to go, so we packed a truck and moved to Colorado with no job prospects. Everyone who knew us thought that this was a ridiculous decision, but we felt it was right. In the end, we both found great jobs and everything worked out for the best. We listened to that inner voice instead of all the outside voices and outside reasoning, even though what our intuition was telling us seemed to be the unwise move to make. Always trust your instinct, even when you can't figure out the logic behind it.

138

We gather the consequences
of our own deeds.
Garuda Purana

You never know when or where the consequences of your actions will come back to you. The law of cause and effect is constant and unfailing. You can always depend on your actions carrying some consequence with them, even if you never see the end result of your action. Also, you never know what string of events your actions will set in motion.

This reminds me of the Zen story of the Zen priest, the young boy, and the horse. The boy's father gave him a horse for his birthday. The boy was very excited and said to the priest, "This is the greatest thing ever!" The priest replied, "Maybe, maybe not. We will see." Later, the boy fell from his horse breaking his leg and could not help the father with his work on the farm. The father said to the priest, "This is terrible. This will ruin my family!" The priest said, "Maybe, maybe not. We will see."

The father was outraged at the priest's lack of concern over his situation. A few days after the incident, the country declared war and all young men the age of his son and older were required to serve in the army and go to war. The boy couldn't go because of his broken leg. Later it was heard that all of the boys from that area that went to battle were slaughtered by the enemy. You never know what events a single action will set into motion. Remember, every little thing matters. Strive to make every action, every word, and every thought right.

139

Only in quiet waters things mirror themselves undistorted. Only in a quiet mind is adequate perception of the world.
Margolis

This sentiment is uttered many times throughout the world's wisdom writings from every culture and part of the world. It is vital that you keep your mind quiet and peaceful. Stress, worry, fear, and the like all distort the mind's perception. You have to keep your mind balanced and think rationally, not allowing emotions to cloud your thinking. Allowing your emotions to cloud your thinking will cause you to make mistakes in both your discernment and your decisions. How can you act right if you can't think right?

You must learn to control your mind. Use meditation to quiet your mind daily. When you feel stress, or your emotions starting to influence your thinking, you can also use a breathing technique called autogenic breathing to calm your mind.

This technique involves inhaling deeply and slowly through your nose for four seconds, holding your breath for three to four seconds, and then exhaling slowly through your mouth for three to four seconds. Autogenic breathing will slow your heart rate, lower your blood pressure, and will relax and calm your mind so you can think clearly. This is an excellent technique to use anytime you start feeling stressed or panicked.

140

One sword keeps another in the sheath.
George Herbert

Many people wonder why warriors spend so much time training when they may never use that training in the real world. One of the answers is put very nicely by George Herbert, "One sword keeps another in the sheath." Even if it appears that the warrior doesn't use his martial arts training in real life, in actuality, he does. No one really knows how many times a violent confrontation has been avoided because of a warrior's training. The confidence that comes from training and the way the warrior presents himself physically, have an effect on the psyche of thugs and ruffians.

Remember, these people always seek to prey on the weak. The bad guys do not want to get into a physical confrontation with someone who appears to be able to defend himself. They would rather bully the guy who looks as if he couldn't win a fight with a wet paper bag. So by this point of view, the warrior uses his martial arts training and other physical training basically daily.

He never knows how many times it has actually been used to deter a predator's attention. Furthermore, he never knows when he will be called on to pull his sword out of the sheath for real, so his sword must be kept sharp and ready. It does little good to carry a sword if you don't know how to use it. Ponder this.

141

There is no first attack in karate.
Gichin Funakoshi

This is a famous martial arts quote from Master Funakoshi, and one which is misinterpreted many times. I have already discussed how the first attack does not necessarily refer to the first physical punch or kick, but rather the first actual threat of danger towards you or those who are under your protection. While this is an important factor to keep in mind when dealing with predators, there is another factor which is equally important in today's society.

It seems that the majority of people in our world today look for the opportunity to sue someone else as a means of getting even or increasing their financial standing. This excessive litigation mentality, along with a lack of common sense in our justice system, has added a whole different dimension to the term self-defense. Self-defense involves more than defending yourself physically.

You have to make sure that you defend yourself in every way. One of the areas that you have to be concerned with is that you are safe from legal prosecution. For this reason, it is sometimes necessary to wait for your enemy to make the first move in order to ensure that witnesses can testify that you have acted in self-defense. Legal prosecution is something to keep in mind.

This is a judgment call which the warrior has to make and many times it has to be made in a split second. Although this is something that you should keep in mind, you cannot let this cause you to put yourself in harm's way. It is a balancing act, and yet another reason for the warrior to think rationally when making important choices during a physical encounter.

142

Our own heart, and not the other men's opinion, forms our true honor.
Samuel Coleridge

Can you really know whether someone else is acting honorably or not? Well, to a certain extent, yes. If someone blatantly lies, cheats, steals, etc. to get his own way or to profit, he is certainly not acting honorably. In many cases it is very easy to see that a man doesn't have any honor. But does this mean that every man who lies or steals is dishonorable? What about a warrior who lies to a drug dealer in an attempt to arrest him and save many kids from the ill effects of the drugs that he is pushing? Is this a dishonorable act just because he lies to this thug? Of course not!

Honor is not black and white. Honor is a complicated ideal which depends on the heart of the person. It depends on his intentions and what is inside. You are not privy to this information and therefore are not in a position to judge the actions of someone else. It is not your place to judge others. It is your duty to keep your honor in place and make sure that you are living according to what is right.

Don't be influenced by the opinions of others. You know in your heart what is right. Only you know if your honor is intact or not. Have the courage to follow your heart, independently of what anyone else says or does. Listen to your conscience. If it tells you that your honor has been compromised, make the necessary changes in your life to set things straight. Don't compromise your honor.

143

Everybody who lives dies.
But not everybody who dies has lived.
Dhaggi Ramanashi

You only live on this earth once, as far as we know, so you better make sure you are living your life to the fullest while you are here. Many people seem to fall into the rut of daily routines only to find that they are walking through life on auto-pilot. They do the same things day after day, never really examining their life or what they want from life. Day by day, month by month, year by year, all pass by quietly until they finally realize that they haven't really lived, they have only stayed alive a bit longer. This is no way for anyone to spend their time on this earth, much less the warrior.

You must take life by the horns and live it to its fullest! Don't waste time. You don't know how much time you actually have, especially if you are a warrior, so you should make the most of every day. Train hard, play hard, love hard, and live life to the fullest. Make sure that when death comes to you, you can say that you have lived a full life and that you have very few regrets. If you don't, I can assure you that you will have many regrets when you look back to all the times that you just walked through life instead of living life.

Live life now! Don't put it off for any reason. Life happens whether you live it or not. You can't stop the sands of the hour glass; they continue to flow no matter what you are doing while they steadily run out. The old saying that it is better to burn out than to rust out is true. The quality of your life counts more than the quantity.

144

Why blast a sparrow with a cannon.
Chinese Proverb

Every situation does not call for the total annihilation of your enemy. The warrior needs to be able to discern how much force is appropriate for different situations. You would not use the same firepower to defend yourself against an attacking mosquito as you would to defend yourself against an attacking elephant. The mosquito is simply a pest, whereas the elephant would be a serious threat to your life.

It would be ridiculous to pull out your high-powered rifle and draw a bead on that mosquito as soon as it landed and squeeze off a round to rid yourself of that pest. You would simply smack it with your hand when it lands on your arm. On the other hand, if you are being attacked by an elephant, I wouldn't recommend using this same method as a form of self-defense. The high-powered rifle would be your only choice other than retreating.

This same principle applies to your self-defense techniques. You have to know the appropriate amount of force to use in each situation. There is no reason to completely annihilate some guy who you know is not an actual physical threat to you, no matter how obnoxious he is being at the time. Even if this guy does attack you, you must use good judgment concerning the danger level. There is a difference in being attacked by someone who couldn't kill the mosquito in the above example, and someone who could give Samson a run for his money. Use good judgment when you have to use your martial arts.

145

Ask questions of your heart, and you will receive answers from your heart.
Omaha Maxim

You must learn to listen to your intuition concerning all things. Meditate and listen to what your heart has to tell you. It will lead you concerning important decisions, but it takes practice to learn to quiet your mind and listen to your heart. This is why you should meditate. Meditation teaches you to control your mind, to quiet the mind and listen to your spirit, and is a vital part of being a warrior. I know that many warriors will disagree with this point and say that this is just mystical mumbo-jumbo, but if you ignore this part of your training, you will be missing an important piece of the warrior's skills.

While it is true that the warrior needs to think rationally in every situation, many times the mind just doesn't know what to do. This is when you must look inside. The spirit does know what to do. It can be hard sometimes, to act on the information that you receive from your heart, because sometimes it can make no sense.

It takes practice to learn to have confidence in your intuition and to listen to what your spirit is guiding you to do. This confidence only comes through practice. This is a skill just like all the other warrior skills and has to be developed in order to be ready for use when it is needed. Practice calming your mind and just listening to your heart throughout the day. Then act on what you hear. Don't just ignore it thinking it is only your thought processes and not really your intuition speaking to you. You have to learn to trust your intuition, and this trust only comes through practice and experience.

146

Do not slide back two paces when you go one step forward.
Sai Baba

The quest to a perfected character is a long and never-ending journey. You have to continually work at this process, and you will have set backs along the way. You have to learn from your mistakes and allow them to teach you lessons that you can use to build your character. At times this process can seem like it is just not working at all.

You may work on controlling your temper and then an hour later you have lost your temper with some obnoxious co-worker. Afterwards the feeling of anger comes up because you know that you have allowed that guy to set you back a step in your quest to perfect your character. You allowed him to control your emotional state. This is why you feel so annoyed when you think back on this incident.

One way to deal with challenges, such as the one above, is to look at those types of situations as "tests." They are tests to see how you will react. When someone is pushing your buttons, see it as part of your training and respond to it as if you are being graded on your performance. Look at it more like a game where the other person is trying to defeat you by annoying you to the point that you explode.

When you explode, you lose the game; he has beaten you. When you look at the situation this way, it takes on a whole different feeling. Play the game to win, and in the process you are also perfecting your character.

147

Betters have their betters.
Japanese Proverb

Don't fall into the trap of believing that you have made it. Don't think that you are the best that there is and nobody else can compete with you. Even if you are the best today, there will be somebody better tomorrow. Nobody is invincible. Nobody is irreplaceable. Even the people who are better than you have people who are better than them. You never reach the point where you are the best, and now you can relax in your training.

This fact is demonstrated every year in sports. One year a team may seem unstoppable. They will destroy their competition week after week, but then the next year, they seem to have lost the magic. Their motivation and their drive to be the best have fallen by the wayside. Things have changed and there is a new "unstoppable" team that has taken over.

We see the same thing in boxing. A fighter may seem undefeatable. He may easily beat everyone who steps into the ring with him. Then one night, he steps into the ring and he is pounded by someone else. He is defeated just as easily as he defeated those who he had fought before.

Don't think that you are indestructible or undefeatable. There is always someone out there who will have more talent and more ability, no matter how good you think you are. You cannot afford to be lax in your training. Keep striving for excellence in every area of your life. There is no such thing as retirement in the warrior lifestyle.

148

At all times, look at the thing itself - the thing behind the appearance.
Marcus Aurelius

The warrior must have enough wisdom to read between the lines. See reality. Don't be fooled by appearances, but rather see things as they really are. This is a rare trait in today's society. Everyone seems to be into appearances, disregarding the truth. People seem to prefer to close their eyes to reality and just be content with nice appearances as long as reality doesn't interfere with their little world.

The warrior is not satisfied with appearances. He has a need to know the truth, and looks beyond the superficial into the realm of reality behind the illusion. He may not be able to change the deceptions that everyone else seems to be alright with, but he at least has the knowledge that he is not fooled by the delusions which the public has accepted as truth.

His insight gives him the knowledge that he needs to protect himself and his family when the truth finally does come forward. He has already seen what is coming and has prepared for the day that the truth, with its consequences, finally does come to light. Always look at someone's motives, not just their presentation. What are their underlying intentions? Look past the carefully scripted and rehearsed stage production that is presented to you. Remember the bait always looks good, but very few see the hidden trap which lies in the shadows.

149

The first law of war is to preserve ourselves and destroy the enemy.
Mao Tse-Tung

Preserve yourself and destroy the enemy. This is what your martial arts training comes down to when you actually need to use it. Yes, it is also about developing your character, but when you get down to the crux of the matter in the street, it boils down to protect yourself and destroy your enemy. This may not be very politically correct, but when you are attacked, it is not time for political correctness. You don't play around. Don't just try to "control" your attacker. One mistake may be all it takes to end your life.

Now, you may be thinking that, "I don't want to hurt this guy that badly. After all, the incident was not that big a deal." Well, here is the bottom line. If it is not important enough or urgent enough to really hurt your enemy, then it is trivial and you should not be engaged in fighting. You should only fight when you have no other choice, and then you should go all out.

If the situation is pressing enough that you have to fight, then it is urgent enough for you to destroy your enemy, period. If it is not that urgent, walk away knowing that you have been the better man and have taken the high road instead of the low road to resolve this situation. Fighting is serious business, not something you do for bragging rights. Once the battle has started, there is no time for second guessing your decision to engage; it is now time for serious business.

150

What is necessary is never a risk.
Cardinal de Retz

This is an interesting quote. At first it seems as if this statement is incorrect. After all, any action can be a risk, right? Well, let's examine that. Is buying groceries for your family a risk? No. Your family has to have food in order to survive. Food is necessary for you and your family. You are not risking your money by buying food. Food is a necessity. But if you went out and bought a new boat with that money, thinking that you would have more income later to buy food, you would be taking a risk. See the difference. A boat is not necessary for your survival, but food is necessary.

The same principle applies to the warrior lifestyle. Some things are necessary for the warrior to live according to the principles by which he has decided to live. Because these traits are necessary for him to stay on the path of the warrior, living up to them is not a risk. The risk is failing to live up to his code of honor. This would not only be a risk to him, but would also be cowering away from his duty, which is unacceptable for a warrior.

Always remember, what is necessary is never a risk; it is simply what has to be done in order to ensure survival. It is necessary for the warrior to walk in honor and integrity. It is necessary for the warrior to take care of his family and protect others. Without doing these things, the warrior would not be able to survive. This doesn't mean that the warrior would die, but simply that there would be no more warrior. Without these warrior traits there is no such thing as the warrior.

151

An enemy surprised is already half-defeated.
German Proverb

I had been working out in a certain dojo, sparring with the same partners over and over, for several months when I decided to start working out with someone new. I spent about a year working out with my new instructor without much contact with my old sparring buddies. One day I got a phone call and was invited back to my old dojo to compete with them in an in-house tournament. It sounded like fun, so I quickly accepted their gracious invitation.

I ended up winning most of my matches that day, much to the disappointment of my old training partners. A great deal of my success had to do with the element of surprise. My buddies were used to my old techniques and maneuvers and thought that they knew what to expect when they were drawn to fight me during the tournament. I could see the confusion on their faces as I countered their attacks with unfamiliar moves. They weren't ready for my new techniques, simply because they had preconceived notions about how I would fight.

Although I am sure that they could handle my new techniques, the change in my style threw them off their game. They allowed the element of surprise to defeat them. It seeded doubt in their minds concerning what I might do next. Small things can make a big difference, especially where the mind is concerned. It doesn't take much to disrupt someone's focus when they are completely surprised, and once their concentration and focus have gone, they are easy to defeat. Use the element of surprise to your advantage; conceal your abilities until you are forced to unveil them.

152

When facing impossible conditions, sometimes it is in your best interest to retreat.
The I Ching

The warrior shouldn't be stubborn, at least not in some areas of his life. When you see conditions have changed, you should change your strategy. Too many people believe that it is their duty to continue on a path once they have started down that path. According to the ancient book of Chinese wisdom, *The I Ching or Book of Changes,* this is wrong thinking. *The I Ching* teaches us that it is not wrong to discard your plans once things have changed.

Parents teach kids that if they start a new sport or hobby, they have to follow through to the end, no matter what. If they find that they don't enjoy it or in fact hate it, people seem to think that it is their duty to make them continue, to teach them not to be quitters. Kids should be taught not to be quitters, but they should also be taught to re-evaluate their goals when things are not working for them.

The same thing is true for warriors. Don't feel you have to fight to the end once you have engaged in a conflict. Sometimes it is in your best interest to retreat and re-evaluate the situation. Always think rationally, not emotionally. Don't continue to fight an impossible battle because of what others may or may not think. Change strategies when they need to be changed. Remember your goal is to protect your life and destroy the enemy, not to "not be a quitter." Do what it takes to achieve your ultimate goal.

153

It is usually the reply that causes the fight.
Japanese Proverb

Always think before you respond to other people. Many people are going to be rude and unfriendly, that is a given. They do not consider other people's feelings. People can be rude and obnoxious, especially when they are drinking, have over-indulged, or are emotionally upset for whatever reason. You are not responsible for the actions of other people. You are responsible for your actions.

You don't have to respond in kind to someone who is acting rude or obnoxious. You can choose to respond kindly, even to the most obnoxious person or you can simply choose to walk away. Don't worry about what others may think about your response; concentrate on making your response appropriate to your standards.

You are not living your life to impress others, but to achieve your goals. It is your goal to live up to your ideals of warriorship. Keep your purpose in mind at all times. Is it your purpose not to allow anyone to mouth off to you or to be rude to you, or is your purpose to live according to your code of ethics?

Determine what your purpose is and then make your decision concerning how to respond to those who do not treat you respectfully. You always have to understand what your ultimate goal is, in order to be able to make the correct decisions to achieve that goal. If you don't know what your destination is, how can you possibly know which road to take to get to your destination?

154

The way is in training.
Do nothing which is not of value.
Miyamoto Musashi

Do nothing which is not of value. This is a strong statement from Miyamoto Musashi, the great Japanese sword master and the author of *The Book of Five Rings*. He is telling us here not to waste our time; to train constantly. I have already discussed how you can basically use anything you do as a form of training, either physically, mentally or spiritually. You determine whether what you are doing is of some real value or whether you are simply wasting time. It totally depends on how you approach what you are doing.

There is absolutely nothing that you can't manipulate into having some value for your training. Okay, I can hear you saying that this is just not true. What about standing in line or sitting in traffic? Well, you can turn both of these into training time. When standing in line, practice being observant of your surroundings. Size people up as you watch them. Notice their mannerisms and study their behavior.

If you are stuck in traffic, it is a perfect time to practice the art of patience and awareness. It is also a good time to practice your breathing techniques. If you think about it, you can convert time which is usually wasted, into valuable training exercises that will help you achieve your goals. Stop wasting time and make whatever you do part of your training. Your time is too valuable to waste.

155

**To expect bad people not to injure
others is crazy. It is to ask the impossible.
And to let them behave like that to other people,
but expect them to exempt you is arrogance.**
Marcus Aurelius

There are bad people in this world, this is a fact. There are sociopaths out there who have no feelings for anyone but themselves. To expect these people to obey the rules of society and respect our laws is ridiculous. They will do harm to others and they will do harm to you, if they are allowed. These people are like the snake in the story of the Farmer and the Snake.

The farmer found a snake out in the cold. It was barely alive, almost frozen to death, so the farmer took off his coat and wrapped the snake in it, and brought the snake into his home to try to save it. He placed the snake by the fireplace, hoping to warm it up and save its life. He cared for the snake until it warmed up and got its strength back.

Then, as the farmer went to check on the snake, the snake lunged and bit the farmer on the neck, rendering a lethal dose of toxic venom. The farmer cried out, "Why would you do this? I saved your life!" As the snake slithered away, it said coldly, "I can't help it. It is just my nature." The farmer died and the snake went on his way.

Don't expect bad people to change their nature and treat you differently than they treat others. As Marcus Aurelius said, that is arrogance, and arrogance can hand you an unexpected defeat. See the true nature of everyone and be prepared for them to act according to their nature.

156

He is wise who tries everything before arms.
Terence

Warriors know that resorting to violence is the last resort. Even though the warrior trains and hones his martial arts skills, and is ready to use them when the occasion demands that he do so, deep inside, he really doesn't want to have to fight. He would much rather talk his way out of situations and settle things peacefully than be forced to hurt someone. For this reason, part of the warrior's training has to focus on ways to resolve conflicts without using his martial arts skills.

The pirates of the 15th and 16th centuries weren't upstanding warriors with honor and integrity, but they did understand the importance of trying to settle things without actually resorting to combat. The pirate flag was a form of psychological warfare. It was meant to discourage sailors from other ships and put fear into their minds. They wanted to win without fighting if possible. Today's warrior should also study these types of techniques.

Exercise your mind as well as your body. Learn negotiation skills and the art of influencing others with your words. Become an expert at calming the emotions of others. Become an expert at psychological warfare. Learn how to plant seeds of fear into your enemy's mind, while at the same time being nice and peaceful. It can be very rewarding to diffuse a volatile situation using only your mind and your words, and ending a conflict without anyone getting hurt.

157

If you have to kill a snake, kill it once and for all.
Japanese Proverb

I have made it clear that the warrior should only use force when it is absolutely necessary. It is not something that the warrior likes to do or is looking forward to having to do, but there are times when the warrior will have no choice. When the time arises and the warrior has no other recourse besides using his martial arts skills, it is important not to hold back. If the situation is serious enough for you to have to resort to violence, it is serious enough for you to totally destroy your enemy.

Now, I'm not saying that every time you have to use your martial arts skills, you should kill your enemy. That is not what I mean by destroying your enemy. What I am saying is that if the situation is serious enough for you to use force, it is serious enough for you to make sure that your enemy cannot do any harm to you, before you consider the conflict to be finished.

If you have to use your martial arts skills, make sure you finish the job. Do not play around. This is not the playground where boys are just pushing and shoving. If that is the situation then you have no business fighting. The warrior only fights when there is no other choice, not for pride or to prove a point. If you have to fight, it is a serious situation, and if it is a serious situation, make sure you take care of business. Make sure that you and those around you are safe when the fight is done.

158

In peace do not forget war.
Japanese Proverb

We live in a fairly peaceful society. Most of us may go our entire lives without having ever been in a real life-or-death conflict. As a rule we don't feel threatened when we go out at night, even in the cities. Because we live in such a peaceful society, we can start to get complacent concerning the need to keep our martial arts skills sharp. But it is important to understand that just because things are peaceful today, doesn't mean that they will always be that way.

You never know when you may have to use your martial arts skills to defend yourself or your loved ones. It could be today or it could be 15 years from now, you just don't know. No one ever really expects to be a target of some thug when they leave home, but every day someone somewhere is mugged. You have to be ready.

The question is, do you want to leave your life up to fate or do you want to make sure that you are ready for whatever may come your way. To the warrior there is no question; it is his duty to be prepared. He cannot afford the luxury of forgetting about war just because everything appears peaceful. He must be prepared for whatever he may encounter. Stay sharp!

159

If we desire to secure peace...it must be known that we are at all times ready for war.
George Washington

Predators prey on the weak or those that they perceive to be weak. As a rule, they do not want to risk attacking someone who appears able to fight back. This is exactly what George Washington was talking about in the quote above. You have a much better chance of the predators not attacking you if it appears that you are able and willing to fight back. They look at the way that you carry yourself, the way you walk, and your overall attitude. Your posture and demeanor can tell people a lot about who you are.

If you desire peace, be peaceful, but at the same time be ready and able to handle conflict should it come to that. Notice that Washington did not say you should *appear* ready for war, but that you *are* ready for war, at all times. You may avoid many problems by your confident appearance and attitude, but you do need to be physically ready to handle an attack if you have to.

Don't just *appear* ready for war; *be* ready for war. Appearances can only take you so far. A bluff only works if no one calls your bluff. It is safer by far, if your appearance of readiness is actually backed up with the skills needed to be ready. Be prepared, to the best of your abilities, to handle whatever situation you may find yourself in during your journey. Be ready for war, even in peace.

160

Bushido, the way of the warrior, is not meant to be self-serving, it is meant to be of service for a higher purpose.

Bohdi Sanders

There are many different aspects which make up bushido, the way of the warrior. This lifestyle encompasses physical, mental, and spiritual facets which are all distinct, yet merge into one to form the character of the true warrior. All of these parts, though different, have one thing in common, they are not for the sole purpose of the warrior himself. The overall character of the true warrior is forged for a higher purpose, that of protecting, helping, and serving others.

The warrior does not seek to perfect his own character in order to brag about how noble he is or in order to impress his friends with his high morals. He does not put in hour after hour of practice time, perfecting his martial arts skills just so he can feel that he is protected when he leaves his home. He does not meditate only to enjoy the bliss of having a quiet mind. All of these practices serve a higher purpose.

This is why the warrior trains so hard. It is his duty to make sure that he is able to protect others. The warrior lifestyle is not an easy road to follow, but it is one which is rewarding for both the warrior and those around him. The warrior's blood, sweat, and tears benefit not only the warrior himself, but every worthy person with whom the warrior comes into contact. Live for a higher purpose; live the warrior lifestyle.

161

Practice not your art and it will soon depart.
German Proverb

It doesn't matter what your art is, if you don't continue to use it and work at it, you will find that your skills have faded. This is true of everything, but it is especially true where your flexibility is concerned. Flexibility is a must for the martial artist. Without flexibility many of your techniques are unusable. The older you get, the more important it is not to allow your daily stretching routine to slide.

It is foundational to your self-defense that you protect yourself, not only from your enemies but also from self-inflicted injuries. If you injure yourself in your training, you certainly won't be prepared to protect yourself on the street, at least not until your injury has had time to heal. Inflexible muscles are easily pulled or torn during a hard martial arts workout, and injuries such as this take a long time to heal properly.

Therefore time spent stretching and increasing your flexibility is vital to your self-defense. As I have said before, everything matters. You can't afford to take any part of your defenses lightly. Stretch daily to develop and maintain flexibility. Don't just half-way go through the motions, but rather concentrate on your muscles as you stretch. See the muscles lengthening and becoming more flexible. Flexibility is the foundation of your martial arts. If your foundation is not solid, everything that you build will be on shaky ground.

162

Honor is sacred.
Native American Maxim

Honor was sacred to the Native American warrior, and honor is sacred to the "real" warrior today. The warrior takes his code of ethics and his character very seriously. If he owes someone a debt, he pays it. If he gives his word, he keeps it. These things are just part of what it means to be a warrior.

During the 1800's the Native Americans were severely mistreated by the United States government. The government continually made treaties with the Native Americans and broke them. They constantly lied to them. One would think that in this environment, the Native Americans would not have considered lying to the government dishonorable, but in the fashion of true warriors, when they gave their word, they kept it.

One Native American warrior, who was captured, convicted of crimes and sentenced to death, pleaded for 30 days in which to prepare for death and see his family. He gave his word that he would return on the 30th day for his punishment. As unbelievable as it sounds, he was granted his 30 days, at which time he was supposed to return for his death sentence to be carried out.

He visited his family, said his good byes, and put his affairs in order. On the 30th day he returned to his captors, lay down on the ground, and was shot in the head. This is an example of a warrior who takes his word of honor seriously. He could have fled and not returned, and he would have lived, but his honor was more sacred than his life.

163

The cherry blossom among flowers, the warrior among men.
Japanese Proverb

Warriors should exhibit the best qualities among men. The true warrior makes a firm decision to try to perfect his character and to live by a strict code of ethics. His word is his honor. His duty stays fresh on his mind. He lives life a little more seriously than most, but at the same time lives life to its fullest. He sees through the veil of appearances covering most parts of this world, but does so without looking down on those who are less perceptive.

Family and friends are important to him, and they know that they can always count on him for protection and help in their times of need. He bases his decisions on his code of ethics, and instinctively knows right from wrong, and chooses right. He knows that at times there is a difference between what is right and what is legal.

The warrior assesses each man by his intentions and actions, rather than his appearance and words. He is able to hold his head high with honor because he knows that he lives his life to the best of his ability, with honor and integrity. His code is ingrained in his spirit and is a part of his being. Warriors walks alone much of the time, as they prefer solitude to the company of lesser men. The warrior truly is the best among men.

164

We love to listen to the old tunes but few today can play the music.
Yamaoka Tesshu

Many men enjoy reading wisdom books and tales of honor and heroism. They fantasize about being men of wisdom, brave and courageous. Some even see themselves as men of honor and think of themselves as warriors. But sadly, most only live by the wisdom and honor that they read about when it is convenient for them to do so. When the chips are down, their bluff is over. They love to listen to the old tunes, but they can't play the music.

The warrior is expected to both listen to the tunes and play the music. He lives the part, where others just play the part. It is like the difference between an actor playing the part of a martial arts expert in a movie, and the martial arts expert in real life. They may appear the same from what you can see on screen, but reality is a different story.

The code of the warrior has to be lived, not just talked about and discussed. There is much to be said for the old ways of the warrior. Morals may change from decade to decade, and from country to country, but the way of the warrior has been a constant ideal of honor and integrity throughout the world for centuries. Don't just listen to the tunes. Learn to play the music, and play it well.

165

No matter how many good words you read and speak of, what good will they do you if you do not put them into practice and use them?
Buddha

This quote from the Buddha really does not need to be expanded on at all. It lays it all on the line for you, plainly and simply. This book contains a lot of wisdom from many sources, but no matter how much you enjoyed reading it, or how many times you read it, it is not worth much in your life if you don't practice what you have learned.

Benjamin Franklin said that reading makes a full man, but meditation makes a profound man. Knowledge without understanding is not worth much. You have to truly understand something in order to be able to use it effectively. The same goes for wisdom. If you only read wise words for entertainment purposes, they may be interesting, but it is not until you truly understand the importance of the concepts that they start to influence your life.

Put the wisdom that you have read in this book into practice in your life. Don't just read it and then forget about it next week. Put it to use and let it help you on your quest to perfect your character. Read and study the wisdom of the elders and let that wisdom change your life. The more that you make the wisdom contained in this book part of your life, the easier it will be for you to make decisions concerning your journey on the path of warriorship. Use your time wisely.

166

If you understand, things are just as they are.
If you do not understand, things are just as they are.
Zen Maxim

See things as they are, not as you want them to be. Things are as they are, whether you look at the reality or the charade. Many people today seem to prefer looking at things through rose colored glasses. Their reality is nothing more than a house of cards. Looking at things through rose colored glasses doesn't change the color of the thing that you are looking at, it only deceives you.

If you look at a white trunk wearing glasses with green lenses, the trunk will appear green, but appearances are deceiving. In this case you have deceived yourself by refusing to take off your colored glasses and seeing the trunk as it truly is. Just because the trunk appears green to you, doesn't change the fact that the trunk is actually white. Refuse to wear colored lenses and begin to see the world as it really is.

Reality is reality, whether you understand it or not. Things do not change just because people wish they were different, or because people refuse to acknowledge the truth. It may be politically correct not to speak the truth, but it does not change the unspoken truth. Truth is truth, whether you acknowledge it or not. Right is right, whether you act on it or not. Things are just as they are. See things as they are, not as someone else wants you to see them. Be perceptive.

167

Moonlight floods the whole sky from horizon to horizon; how much it can fill your room depends on your windows.
Rumi

There has been a lot of wisdom presented in this book. How much of it has entered your consciousness depends on you. The sun lights up the whole earth, but if you stay in your basement and cover your windows with dark blankets, it cannot light your basement and you will not see the sun or benefit from its light.

The same goes for the wisdom presented in this book. You have to allow it to penetrate your mind in order to get any benefit from it. If you don't meditate on it and don't absorb it into your consciousness, it will not profit you. Even though there has been a lot of wisdom offered to you, you have to take it and use it or it is worthless to you.

If I were to offer you $1,000 and you refused to take the money and invest it or spend it, then it would be completely worthless to you. But if you were to take that $1,000 and invest it carefully, watch over it, protect it, and continue to add to it, it would benefit you for years to come. The same principle applies to the wisdom contained in this book. Plant it in your mind, cultivate it, watch over it, meditate on it, and continue to add to it, and it will benefit you for the rest of your life.

168

It is you who must make the effort; the sages can only teach.
The Dhammapada

There are volumes of wisdom and teachings from around the world and throughout the centuries that can help you on your path to warriorship. Read and study all you can. Work at developing your character and your integrity. When you fall short, and you most likely will at some point, don't quit. Just acknowledge that you missed it and continue on your quest. Nobody is perfect.

It takes effort, a lot of effort, to live the lifestyle of the warrior, but it is worth it. Nothing worthwhile comes easy. You have to work at it daily. If you don't make the effort to apply what you have learned, then what good has it done you? Don't procrastinate, start applying what you have studied today and make it your daily lifestyle.

Don't just read through this information once. Reading this wisdom once is not sufficient enough to make changes in your life. You must study it and apply it to your life. The path of the warrior requires action, not merely the thought of action. It does no good to *think* about helping someone in need, you have to *actually help* that person. Be a man of action and use what you have learned.

The Martial Way does not start and end at the door of the training hall. It is a way of life in which every action, in and out of the training hall, is done in the context of warriorship...

The Martial Way is a way of living. It is a holistic discipline aimed at the pursuit of excellence, not just in the training hall, but at life. Its disciples strive to apply the Way in every vocation, and its adepts tend to be achievers in any field of endeavor...

One lives The Martial Way.

Forrest E. Morgan

Afterword

Thank you for your purchase of *Warrior Wisdom*. I hope that you found the wisdom contained within to be useful in your life and for your goals as you travel along the path of the warrior. Please remember, that for this wisdom to truly become a part of you, you have to internalize it, meditate on it and keep it fresh in your mind. Wise words are only concepts. You must go beyond the concepts and actually experience the effects of the wisdom in your life.

I sincerely hope that you refer back to *Warrior Wisdom* often and continue to meditate on the guidance provided by the many wise words it contains. Simply reading through this book once is not enough to make the wisdom it contains yours; you have to go past the reading, to a place of deep understanding for the wisdom to actually be useful. It is the fruits of the warrior lifestyle that are important, not the philosophy alone. All you learn and all you read is of little use to you if it doesn't produce real changes in your life.

Theodore Parker stated, "The books that help you most are those which make you think the most." It is my fondest hope that by reading and then implementing what you have read in *Warrior Wisdom,* that it will have had a profound and positive impact on your life. Hopefully, *Warrior Wisdom* has made you think about how you should live your life and the benefits of living the warrior lifestyle.

I would love to hear your feedback on *Warrior Wisdom*. What do you feel about what you have read? Did you find it helpful? Please send your comments to me by e-mail to: WarriorWisdom@comcast.net. Also please put "Feedback" in the heading.

Live with honor!

Bohdi Sanders, PhD

Appendix

Aeschylus – (525 BC–455 BC), ancient Greek playwright. He is often recognized as the father or the founder of tragedy.

Aesop – 6th century Greek author of Aesop's Fables.

Aristotle – (384 BC–322 BC), Greek philosopher, a student of Plato and teacher of Alexander the Great.

Aurelius, Marcus – (121–180), was Roman Emperor from 161 to his death in 180. He was the last of the "Five Good Emperors" and is also considered one of the most important Stoic philosophers.

Baba, Sai – South Indian guru, religious leader, orator.

Bacon, Francis – (1561–1626), English philosopher, statesman, and essayist.

Basho – (1644–1694), the most famous poet of the Edo period in Japan.

Bhagavad Gita – An ancient Sanskrit text.

Bodhidharma – Buddhist monk traditionally credited for bringing martial arts to China.

Bonaparte, Napoleon – (1769–1821), French military and political leader who had significant impact on modern European history. He was a general during the French Revolution, and the ruler of France.

Buddha – (563 BC–483 BC), spiritual teacher from ancient India and the founder of Buddhism.

Bushido Shoshinshu – Samurai text written by Taira Shigesuke around 1700. Its purpose was to instruct the novice Samurai of the peaceful Edo Era, who had not known the rigors of battle, with the practical philosophies of previous eras.

Cardinal de Retz – (1614–1679), French churchman and writer.

Cervantes, Miguel de – (1547–1616), was a Spanish novelist, poet, painter and playwright. Cervantes is one of the most important and influential people in literature and the author of the novel *Don Quixote.*

Chesterson, G. K.– (1874–1936), well known writer and lecturer.

Chu, F. J. – Martial artist and author of *The Martial Way and its Virtues.*

Code of the Samurai – A Modern Translation of the *Bushido Shoshinshu.*

Coleridge, Samuel – (1772–1834), English poet, critic, and philosopher.

Confucius – (551 BC–479 BC), Chinese thinker and social philosopher, whose teachings and philosophy have deeply influenced Chinese, Korean, Japanese, and Vietnamese thought and life.

Dalai Lama – leader who presides over the Central Tibetan Administration. He is often referred to simply as "His Holiness."

Deshimaru, Taisen – (1914–1982), Japanese Soto Zen Buddhist teacher. Born in the Saga Prefecture of Kyushu, Deshimaru was raised by his grandfather, a former Samurai before the Meiji Revolution.

The Dhammapada – a Buddhist scripture, containing 423 verses in 26 categories. According to tradition, these are verses spoken by the Buddha on various occasions, most of which deal with ethics.

Dogen – (1200–1253), Japanese Zen Buddhist teacher born in Kyôto, and the founder of the Sôtô school of Zen in Japan.

Emerson, Ralph Waldo – (1803–1882), American essayist, philosopher, poet, and leader of the Transcendentalist movement in the early 19th century.

Epictetus – (55–135), Greek Stoic philosopher.

Funakoshi, Gichin – (1868–1957), founder of Shotokan karate and is attributed as being the "father of modern karate."

Furuya, Kensho – Martial artist, chief instructor of the Aikido Center in Los Angeles.

Garuda Purana – is one of the Puranas which are part of the Hindu body of texts known as the Smriti.

Gracian, Baltasar – (1601–1658), Spanish Baroque prose writer.

Guicciardini, Francesco – (1483–1540), Italian historian and statesman. He is considered one of the major political writers of the Italian Renaissance.

Hagakure – Japanese text for the warrior, drawn from a collection of commentaries by the samurai, Yamamoto Tsunetomo.

Hatsumi, Masaaki – Founder and current head of the Bujinkan Dojo martial arts organization.

Herbert, George – Welsh poet, orator and a priest.

Hobart, Peter – Martial artist and author of *Kishido: The Way of the Western Warrior.*

I Ching – also called *Book of Changes* or *Classic of Changes* is one of the oldest of the Chinese classic texts.

Juan, Don – Yaqui Indian Shaman.

Lee, Bruce – (1940–1973), American-born martial artist, philosopher, instructor, martial arts actor and the founder of the Jeet Kune Do martial arts system.

Margolis – Native American leader.

Moliere – (1622–1673), French playwright and actor.

Montaigne, Michel – (1533–1592), one of the most influential writers of the French Renaissance.

Morgan, Forrest E. – Martial artist and author of *Living the Martial Way*.

Musashi, Miyamoto – (1584–1645), Japanese swordsman famed for his duels and distinctive style.

Nagarjuna – (150–250), Indian philosopher, the founder of the Madhyamaka (Middle Path) school of Mahâyâna Buddhism, and arguably the most influential Buddhist thinker after Gautama Buddha himself.

Nai'an, Shi – (1296–1372), was a classical Chinese author.

Osborne, Sir Frances – (1751–1799), 5th Duke of Leeds.

Ovid – (43BC–AD 17), Publius Ovidius Naso, Roman poet.

Oyama, Masutatsu – (1923–1994), also known as Mas Oyama, was a karate master who founded Kyokushinkai, arguably the first and most influential style of full contact karate.

Panchatantra – An Indian work of morally enlightening tales in Sanskrit originating around the year 500.

Pandit, Sakya – (1182–1251), Tibetan scholar.

Pythagoras – Greek mathematician and philosopher.

Roosevelt, Franklin Delano – (1882–1945), often referred to by his initials FDR, was the thirty-second President of the United States.

Rumi – (1207–1273), 13th century Persian poet, Islamic jurist, and theologian.

Seizen, Matsura – (1646–1713), martial artist, teacher and swordsman.

Shakespeare, William –(1564–1616), English poet and playwright, widely regarded as the greatest writer in the English language.

Skinner, Dirk – Martial artist and author of *Street Ninja*.

Soho, Takuan – (1573–1645), a major figure in the Rinzai school of Zen Buddhism.

Spinoza, Baruch – (1632–1677), Dutch philosopher of Portuguese Jewish origin. Today, he is considered one of the great rationalists of 17th-century philosophy, laying the groundwork for the 18th-century Enlightenment.

Spurgeon, Charles – (1834–1892), British Reformed Baptist preacher.

Stanhope, Philip Dormer – (1694–1773), British statesman.

Suzuki, Shunryu – (1904–1971), Soto Zen priest born in the Kanagawa Prefecture of Japan.

Tabata, Kazumi – Martial artist and author of "Secret Tactics." Taylor,

Bayard – (1825–1878), U.S. poet and writer.

Tecumseh – (1768–1813), famous Shawnee leader. He spent much of his life attempting to rally Native American tribes in defense of their lands, which eventually led to his death in the War of 1812.

Terence – (185 BC–195 BC), playwright of the Roman Republic.

Tesshu, Yamaoka – famous Samurai living during the period known as the Meiji Restoration.

Thoreau, Henry David – (1817–1862), American author, naturalist, transcendentalist.

Thurber, James – (1894–1961), American writer.

Tiruvalluvar – 2nd century BC Tamil poet who wrote the Thirukkural, a well-known ethical work in Tamil literature.

Toshisada, Kotoda Yahei – 18th century martial artist and author. Ts'an,

Seng – 6th century Buddhist layman.

Tse-Tung, Mao – (1893–1976), Chinese military and political leader.

Tzu, Lao – 6th century BC philosopher of ancient China and is a central figure in Taoism.

Tzu, Sun – (544 BC–496 BC), the author of *The Art of War*, an immensely influential ancient Chinese book on military strategy.

Vegetius – Writer during the Later Roman Empire.

Washington, George – (1732–1799), the first President of the United States, after leading the Continental Army to victory over the Kingdom of Great Britain in the American Revolutionary War (1775–1783).

Zheng, Wei – (580–643), Chinese politician and the lead editor of the *Book of Sui*, composed in 636. He served as a chancellor of Tang Dynasty.

Index

178

Other Titles by Bohdi Sanders

Secrets of the Soul is a guide to uncovering your deeply hiden beliefs. This delightful book provides over 1,150 probing questions which guide you to a thorough understanding of who you are and what you believe. Take this unbelievably entertaining journey to a much deeper place of self-awareness. Where do your beliefs come from? Do you really know exactly what you believe and why you believe it? You will after reading **Secrets of the Soul**. This book will help you uncover your true beliefs!

WARRIOR is the second book in the **Warrior Wisdom Series**. Wisdom, life-changing quotes, and entertaining, practical commentaries fill every page. This series has been recognized by four martial arts hall of fame organizations for its inspirational and motivational qualities. The ancient and modern wisdom in this book will definitely help you improve your life and bring meaning to each and every day. The USMAA Hall of Fame awarded Dr. Sanders with Inspiration of the Year for this series!

The Warrior Lifestyle is the last installment of the award winning **Warrior Wisdom Series**. Forwarded by martial arts legend Loren W. Christensen, this book has been dubbed as highly inspirational and motivational. If you want to live your life to the fullest, you need to read this one! Don't settle for an ordinary life, make your life extraordinary! The advice and wisdom shines on every page of this book, making it a must read for everyone who strives to live an extraordinary life of character and honor!

Other Titles by Bohdi Sanders

Wisdom of the Elders is a unique, one-of-a-kind quote book. This book is filled with quotes that focus on living life to the fullest with honor, character, and integrity. Honored by the USA Book News with a 1st place award for Best Books of the Year in 2010, this book is a guide for life. *Wisdom of the Elders* contains over 4,800 quotes, all which lead the reader to a life of excellence. If you enjoy quotes, wisdom, and knowledge, you will love this book. This is truly the ultimate quote book for those searching for wisdom!

Defensive Living takes the reader deep into the minds of nine of the most revered masters of worldly wisdom. It reveals valuable insights concerning human nature from some of the greatest minds the world has ever known, such as Sun Tzu, Gracian, Goethe, and others. *Defensive Living* presents invaluable lessons for living and advice for avoiding the many pitfalls of human relationships. This is an invaluable and entertaining guidebook for living a successful and rewarding life!

Modern Bushido is all about living a life of excellence. This book covers 30 essential traits that will change your life. *Modern Bushido* expands on the standards and principles needed for a life of excellence, and applies them directly to life in today's world. Readers will be motivated and inspired by the straightforward wisdom in this enlightening book. If you want to live a life of excellence, this book is for you! This is a must read for every martial artist and anyone who seeks to live life as it is meant to be lived.

Looking for More Wisdom?

If you are interested in living the warrior lifestyle or simply in living a life of character, integrity and honor you will enjoy The Wisdom Warrior website and newsletter. The Wisdom Warrior website contains dozens of articles, useful links, and news for those seeking to live the warrior lifestyle.

The newsletter is also a valuable resource. Each edition of The Wisdom Warrior Newsletter is packed with motivating quotes, articles, and information which everyone will find useful in their journey to perfect their character and live the life which they were meant to live.

The Wisdom Warrior Newsletter is a newsletter sent directly to your email account and is absolutely FREE! There is no cost or obligation to you whatsoever. You will also receive the current news updates and new articles by Dr. Bohdi Sanders as soon as they are available. Your email address is never shared with anyone else.

All you need to do to start receiving this valuable and informative newsletter is to go to the Wisdom Warrior website and simply sign up. It is that simple! You will find The Wisdom Warrior website at:

www.TheWisdomWarrior.com

Also, be sure to find posts by Dr. Sanders on Facebook. Dr. Sanders posts enlightening commentaries, photographs, and quotes throughout the week on his Facebook pages. You can find them at:

www.facebook.com/The.Warrior.Lifestyle

www.facebook.com/EldersWisdom

www.facebook.com/bohdi.sanders

Don't miss the opportunity to receive tons of FREE wisdom, enlightening posts, interesting articles, and intriguing photographs on The Wisdom Warrior website and on Dr. Sanders' Facebook pages.

Sign Up Today!

9382417R00116

Made in the USA
San Bernardino, CA
14 March 2014